My Man My Abuser
Rocky Rose

I0187333

Dedication

This book is dedicated to my Aunt Sara Katherine Rose who was taken from me before we had the chance to meet one another. I'm often told I act just like her and my attitude resembles hers, which in my opinion isn't a bad thing. Even though we never got the opportunity to meet one another, I love you beyond words Aunt Kat, until we meet, your niece Rocky.

I'm also dedicating this book to two of my Uncles, James Rose and Glen Senior. The both of you always backed my decision to write, you encouraged me to do it when others told me I was crazy for thinking I could be a writer. I love you both; I miss the hell out of the both of you. I'm going to make you proud!

Acknowledgments

First and foremost I have to thank my Lord and Savior Jesus Christ for granting me the wonderful gift of writing and the imagination to bring the voices of the characters to life through print.

My baby girl Ajia, even though it'll be quite a few years before you pick up any of my books to read, I want you to know that it is because of you that I grind as hard as I do. You coming into my life May 2009 began my life as a person all around. I started these two businesses to show you that if you put your mind to doing something and you keep God as your pilot, you can accomplish anything! I love you unconditionally, I will always have your back, I will support you in whatever you decide to do and know that you will always be #1 in my heart!

I have to thank my brother-in-law Larry and sister LaVona, I love you both and I appreciate you from the bottom of my heart for helping me with my daughter whenever I needed you. I owe the both of you big time!

My big *cousin* Tya, I love you for who you are. You've seen me grow from a little girl into the woman I am today; you know my struggles, my strengths and my story. You understand me better than most people who see me on a daily basis. I thank you from the bottom of my heart for being who you are, you are truly a blessing to me, and you ROCK! One with God One with Self!

Mr. Denby, words can't express how I feel about you and how much I thank you for being in my corner. I love you and thank you for being you. Hopefully we will continue on this journey. I thank you for the support you've shown me since we've met; you encourage me to do better and grind harder.

Old head, you've been a supporter of my career from the very beginning and you've also been a pain from the very beginning but through it all I appreciate the support you've shown me. Our friendship isn't as strong as it used to be but nonetheless I appreciate the support. Thank you!

Allyson Deese, I thank you for being a sister, a friend and my graphic designer for this book, so many people love both covers as do I. I love you for being you and for the support!

My editor, Tiff Jasper, thank you!! You came highly recommended by Treasure Blue and I think that says a lot about you as a businesswoman. I appreciate the time and effort you put into editing this manuscript for me; trust me, we will be doing more business together in the future!

Treasure Blue and Allison Edwards, I humbly thank you both for your help, advice and honesty when it comes to helping newbie's in the writing/publishing business. Our time to meet in person is coming soon. The both of you are passionate about your craft and you take time out of your schedules to assist others as they pursue their dream of becoming writers and authors, thank you from the bottom of my heart.

To all of my family and supporters, I thank each and every one of you! This book has taken me years to write and I know a lot of my family and those close to me have been waiting for its release for a long time now, but it's finally here.

Take a seat, relax, grab a drink and take this ride with Qortni and Qamar in My Man My Abuser.

I used to give a fuck, then I stopped; you see the life of a pastor's child is not all it's cracked up to be. I'm not perfect, shit far from it to be real.

My name is Qortni Monroe; I'm nineteen years old from New Haven, one of the meanest cities in Connecticut, I recently dropped out of college 'cause I couldn't keep my scholarship money and change my major so I decided to just quit. I didn't just quit and do nothing with my life; I enrolled into a writing program that was strictly for writing and breaking into print.

In 2004, a year after graduating from high school I met this guy by the name of Qamar Daniels and we began chatting through BlackPlanet, then Yahoo Messenger, then finally meeting in person.

On October 19, 2004, Qamar and I made it official, we officially became a couple. I officially was in a relationship with Satan himself and I wasn't even aware of what I was getting myself into. It still amazes me how someone can make himself or herself appear to be the best thing since sliced bread, but in all actuality they're the worst things since women getting their period once a month.

In the beginning everything between Qamar and I was real cool, conversations were always on point, we'd fall asleep on the phone with one another, 'cause neither one of us wanted to be the first to hang up; yeah, I used to do corny shit like that. Anyhow, his friends seemed to like me, as I think back on it now, maybe they liked me a little too much back then; they had a very unique way of getting to know me, a way that I didn't think too much of, and didn't think anything was wrong with how we began getting to know one another.

"So, Qortni, what's your sign?" Asked Qamar's cousin Nathan,

"I'm a sexy Gemini."

"Cool, what's your favorite position?"

"Doggy style, all day every day."

"Damn, how come I couldn't have met you first? I don't think Qamar will know what to do with you or how to handle you, real talk," chimed in Nature.

Just as Nature was about to ask me a question, Qamar called for me.

"Qortni, let me holla at you for a minute," he said with a hint of aggravation in his voice.

"Excuse me guys, I'll be right back."

I left Nature and Nathan sitting on Qamar's sun porch and made my way into Qamar's mother's house.

"What's up bae? How come you sound irritated and mad?"

"Why the fuck are you out there telling these guys your favorite positions like it's all good?"

"They asked and I answered."

"You don't see anything wrong with you telling that type of shit to my cousin and peoples?"

"What the fuck is the big problem? You're acting like I'm outside fucking them; they're asking me questions, and I'm answering. What? You want me to not answer the questions when they ask me?" I asked with my hands on my hips and my neck rolling.

"Don't you ever again in your life disrespect me like that again, do you understand me? If they ask you questions like that, you better tell them that you are not at liberty to divulge that type of information, do we understand each other?"

I began laughing, was he serious? "Last time I checked, I was a grown ass woman, I don't have a ring on my left ring finger, so if anyone wanted to ask me what ever questions they feel as they want an answer to, I will answer."

"You must think I'm joking," he said getting into my face and stepping into my personal space.

"I never said you were joking, but I want you to realize that as long as I'm not sucking their dicks or fucking them, I'm not being disrespectful. I'm merely having an adult conversation with them; now chill the fuck out," I told him before walking back out to the sun porch.

Nathan and Nature must've heard the conversation Qamar and I were having and thought it would be best if they left because they were nowhere in sight when I got back to the porch.

Being that they left, I decided to get my bag and bounce as well. Qamar really had some shit with him, so instead of staying over any longer I just thought it best to give him his time to cool off. I stepped into his mother's kitchen and as soon as I turned the corner into the kitchen, I was knocked on my ass, courtesy of Qamar and his left fist,

"What the fuck is your problem? Why in the hell did you punch me? Are you out of your mind?" I asked with the most perplexed look on my face.

"Oh, you must have thought you were goin' to have the last word and just go on about your business?"

"Do you realize you just put your fucking hands on me? Do you realize that by doing that you just signed your own death certificate? You spoke your piece, I spoke mine, and I waked away, end of story."

"Nah shorty, it's not the end of the story 'til I say so," he told me, having the audacity to try and help me up.

I pushed his hand away, getting up off the floor by myself; I went to his mother's bathroom and noticed my left eye was beginning to swell. I retrieved my bag from the kitchen and started to walk to the front door, but noticed Qamar sitting on his mother's couch with tears flowing freely from his eyes. I didn't want to stop and ask what his problem was, but seeing him cry, the little angel on my shoulder told me not to be cold and ask him if he was all right.

"What's the matter Q?"

"Shorty, I apologize for putting my hands on you, I did it out of frustration, and I allowed my frustrations to get the best of me," he replied wiping the tears from the corners of his eyes.

"I'm not going to say that you putting your hands on me is cool, 'cause it's damn sure not. I've been thinking about our relationship for a while, and I think one of two things need to happen. One, we can take some time off from one another, or two we can go to counseling to work through our problems with the help of someone professional."

"I definitely don't want to take any time off 'cause that'll open up the possibility of you meeting some other guy, I ain't even trying to hear that. On the flip side, I don't want to go to some shrink who will start judging me the moment I open my mouth to them. We'll just work through our problems together."

I wasn't agreeing with his reasoning but I thought it best to keep my mouth shut 'cause I really didn't want my right eye to match my left.

"How about we both sleep on our options and come to some type of conclusion in a day or so?"

"I have already made my decision shorty, I just told you that."

"Fine Q, I won't argue with you. Listen, I'm about to head on home, I'm tired and my head is pounding," I told him while standing up and grabbing my bag off his mother's sofa.

"Aight shorty, call me when you get in, I'll have my phone on, but I'm about to link back up with Nature and Nathan."

"Okay, talk to you later," I responded while making my way to his mother's front door.

As I was leaving, I looked at my eye and noticed it was full-fledged black and on the verge of swelling shut.

I tried my best to style my hair so that when I walked into my house no one would notice my eye. I didn't want to have to explain to all the nosy ass people in that house why my face looked like I lost a fight to Mike Tyson.

As soon as I got in the house, I went to my room, grabbed my pajama pants, a tank top, my robe and a towel, and made my way to the shower. I made sure to put the lock on the bathroom door 'cause some people in this house have no type of common courtesy and will just barge into the bathroom to either pee, shit, or just to converse. Now, correct me if I'm wrong, but family or not, it's never politically correct for any family member, male or female, to ever just feel free to utilize the bathroom while I'm in the shower. I pinned my hair up and just stared at my eye, which was black and completely shut; I swear I wanted to kill Qamar for doing this shit to me.

I put my iPod in the dock, selected my slow jams playlist, then stepped in the shower and allowed the hot water to relax me. As I was washing up I heard banging on the bathroom door, it was my mother asking if she could use the bathroom. I told her I'd be out in a little while, but she wasn't trying to hear that.

"Qortni, take the lock off the door, I'll be in and out in less than five minutes, now unlock the door!"

I cut my shower short, turned off the water and music, grabbed my towel, and almost took the lock off the door until I caught a glimpse of my black eye in the mirror.

"Qortni, what in the world are you doing in there? Open the door, I'm about to pee on myself."

"I'll be out in a minute, damn, I didn't know it was a crime to take a shower without interruptions around here. You do realize there's a bathroom upstairs with a working toilet," I replied to her while fixing my hair to cover my eye.

When I finally opened the door my mother gave me a look that would've killed me if looks could kill. As soon as she got in the bathroom and shut the door, she asked why I had the lock on the door in the first place and what took me so long to unlock it and let her in.

"I already told you it would be nice if I could take a shower uninterrupted and undisturbed once in a while. Who wants to take a shower with someone pissing in the toilet? The whole time you were standing out here waiting for me, you could have gone upstairs and used that bathroom up there."

"I don't live upstairs, I live down here, so I'll use this bathroom whenever I damn well please. You don't pay any bills around here so next time you decided to lock a door around here, be prepared for me to take tit off the hinges," she said with much attitude.

"It's not that serious in the first place, I know you can't stand being interrupted when you're in the shower or tub so what makes you think I want to be? Just have some respect and consideration for everyone in the house just like you want us to have for you, is that asking too much?"

"I'll have some consideration when you start paying some bills around here."

I laughed, whom did she think she was kidding? "Well, you don't pay any bills around here either so looks like we're in the same boat now doesn't it?" I responded to her.

I was getting fed the fuck up with her attitude, walking around here like she owns this house or something, when in fact her and my father pay my aunt rent every month to stay here.

"I don't know what your problem is, but whatever it is, you need to fix it. Don't think for a moment that just because you're nineteen years old means you're too grown to get the taste knocked out of you. I'm not one of your friends on the outside, I'm your mother and you will respect me as such, do I make myself clear?" she asked opening the bathroom door and stepping into my personal space.

I didn't even bother to respond, I merely walked away from her 'cause if the answer that was on the tip of my tongue slipped out, there was no question in my mind that she and I would have come to blows and I have already had enough of that type of excitement for one day.

When I got up to my room, I noticed Qamar had called and texted me a total of ten times. I honestly didn't feel like being bothered by him tonight, I just wanted to relax, pen a couple of pages in my journal and vibe out to my music until I fell asleep. Instead of returning any of his calls or messages, I decided to put my phone on silent and just enjoy the quiet time I most definitely needed.

Qamar

I can't believe Qortni isn't answering any of my calls or messages, can't believe she didn't even hit my jack to let me know she made it to her crib safely. I know I was fucked up for putting my hands on her, but her smart-ass mouth got me vexed, and instead of walking away like I should have, I brought her to the school of Ike Turner.

Was I wrong? Absolutely, and I'll openly admit that to y'all but I'd never admit it to Qortni; my pride level is ridiculously high. She really pissed me off earlier though, like really, what chick in their right mind would openly tell their man's friends what her favorite positions are and how good they are at giving head? She totally disrespected me and I had to check her ass. Did I mean to hit her as hard as I did? Absolutely not, but shit happens.

After she bounced I called Nathan and Nature to see what they were getting into for the night 'cause I was damn sure not trying to stay in the house.

"Yo, Q, ya shorty dipped? Nate and I heard the both of you going at it and we weren't tryin' to get in the middle of that shit," Nature asked me.

"Yeah, she bounced. What y'all getting into tonight? I'm not trying to stay home tonight."

"I don't know about Nate, but I'm chillin' with my shorty right now, and most likely the rest of the evening."

'Aight, well, you get back to your shorty, I'm going to call Nate and see what he's doing for the night."

"Aight black, I'll link up with y'all tomorrow."

"Bet."

After getting off the phone with Nature, I tried reaching Nathan but to no avail, and I found it kind of odd that neither Qortni nor Nathan were answering their phones; I prayed that they weren't somewhere together, 'cause that wouldn't be a good look for either one them, real shit.

I decided to play the crib for the evening since Nature was with his shorty and Nate was nowhere to be found. I hopped on the Nintendo 64 and started playing Golden Eye 007. I was getting into my game until I got a message on my phone from my homegirl Talisha. She and I have been cool for damn near our whole lives, just from growing up in the same hood. Qortni and Talisha don't really get along. Qortni thinks that for some reason or another Talisha has some feelings for me, but I highly doubt it, at least I haven't gotten that vibe from her.

I read the message from Talisha and she said that Qortni was at Van Dome nightclub and had a bunch of guys around her. As soon as I read that, I didn't even bother to text her back, I got dressed, got in my aunt's car and made a mad dash to the club; no wonder why Qortni wasn't answering my calls or messages. I guess me punching her earlier wasn't enough for her ass; guess I'll have to show her ass a thing or two tonight.

Qortni

E very so often while I was listening to my music and writing, I'd glance at my phone and this one particular time I glanced at it and noticed my cousin Amberlin sent me a message about going out with her; my initial thought was to ignore her, but then I thought about who I was dealing with and if I didn't respond to her she'd end up coming over to the crib, no matter what time it is. I texted her back and told her I'd have to decline because I wasn't feeling too well and I was already in bed.

Instead of texting me back, Amber called me.

"Damn bitch, it's only a little after ten and you're in bed already? I was hoping we could do our infamous twin prank we always do."

"Not tonight chica, maybe next weekend, I just need to vibe out to my music and write tonight, got too much on my mind to be in anyone's club shakin' my ass."

"Alright chica; oh, before I forget, do you have a sweater dress I can borrow? I bought these banging ass ankle boots today from the mall and I need a cute, form fitting dress to go with them."

"I actually have a grey one you can have, I haven't even popped the tags off of it yet, it's getting a little snug on me some reason."

"You don't mind giving it to me? I just need it for tonight."

"I don't mind at all, you can come to the crib now and get it if you like."

"Okay, I'll call you when I get outside."

"Bet."

Amberlin's mother and my father are siblings but if you didn't know any better you'd think her and I were twins. Twins run in our family, my grandmother and grandfather both come from families where twins are common; I always said I wanted at least two sets of twins, a set of boys and a set of girls. If Qamar and I stay together long enough to procreate we'll have about a one hundred and fifty percent chance of having twins because twins run in his family as well.

Back before Qamar and I started dating, Amberlin and I would dress alike and paint the town red, making guys really believe we were twins, and now that I think about it, I miss those days. We would have guys heads all messed up, I remember one time we had this guy thinking he had slept with me when in fact he really slept with her, yeah those were definitely the days.

Amber sent me a text when she got in front of my house 'cause she was on the phone with her boo of the month so I put on some shorts, grabbed the dress from my closet, and met her at her car. I took it upon myself to let myself in her car without getting an official invitation' and waited 'til she finished talking to her dude.

"So trick, are you really staying in the house tonight or are you linking up with someone other than Qamar?"

"Bitch, what did I tell you? I'm staying in, vibing to my music and writing until I fall asleep. I ain't checking for no one but Qamar," I told her as gently placed my right hand over my right eye that was swollen shut.

"Qort, what's wrong with your eye?"

"Nothing, I just have a terrible migraine that's all," I told her in a voice that even I would not have believed.

She turned my face towards her and pushed my hair back off my eye.

"Qort, what the hell happened to your face? And don't even bother trying to lie to me."

"Q and I got into and argument earlier today and he allowed his emotions to get the best of him and socked me clean in my face," I told her while repositioning my hair to cover my eye again.

"Please tell me that punk ass dude isn't still breathing, please tell me he's in someone's body bag."

"Amber please, yes he's still breathing, it's not totally his fault, and I did kind of provoke him to do this."

"Qort, there is never, and I repeat never a viable excuse for a man to put his hands on a female in a violent manner, I don't give a fuck what words may have been exchanged or even if you muffed him in the head, there's no excuse for your face to be looking like that."

"This is the exact conversation I've been trying to avoid with everyone since this shit happened," I told my cousin while opening the car door.

"Qortni, I'm coming over to scoop you in the morning, we're not done talking yet; we need to have a serious one on one, heart to heart talk."

"Aight, just call me when you wake up and we can make moves from there."

"All right chica, love you," she told me as we embraced in a hug.

"Love you too mama."

Amberlin

When I saw my cousin's eye I immediately wanted to kill whomever was responsible for doing that to her. When she told me it was Qamar who put his hands on her, I wanted to murder him instantly.

You see, Qamar and I have never gotten along, even before him and Qortni met and started dating. Qamar is best friends to one of my ex-boyfriends, and even back then, his aura always seemed a bit off to me, and I could never put my finger on why, that is until I saw my cousin's eye this evening, it was at that very moment after she told me he did it, that a light bulb came on I then realized that Qamar has a serious issue with controlling his temper and keeping his hands to himself. Qortni and I were always taught by our grandmother that if a man hits you while you're dating, first of all he's not a real man and second of all he'll kill you after the both of you say 'I do'.

I've never been a fan of domestic violence, just seems to me if a man hits a woman so nonchalantly, he must be a punk, 'cause I can bet any amount of money he wouldn't dare hit a man so quickly. I honestly don't know what my cousin sees in Qamar, 'cause he's not attractive, he has no job has no set goals for his life, and he's just a bum. From what Qortni tells me, he is absolutely terrible in bed, like his dick is the size of my pinky finger, I just don't get it; he must have some type of mind control over Qort for her to be putting up with that hitting bullshit.

As soon as I got to the Van Dome I made a mad dash to the bar and ordered myself two shots of Hennessey, a shot for each hand. I needed to calm my nerves down 'cause it was taking everything in me not to hunt Qamar's punk ass down and beat him to pulp, visions of Qortni's eye still played in my memory, that shit was crazy.

As I was standing at the bar the dress Qortni gave me was definitely doing it's job 'cause every few seconds a random guy would ask me if I wanted more shots of Henney, and of course I didn't turn them down;

that would have been plain rude of me, and I'm definitely not the rude type.

I was downing shots nine and ten and I kept feeling someone staring at me so I smoothly put my back towards the bar and I scanned the club to see who was trying to burn a hole through me with their eyes, but I came up empty handed. When I was about to order myself an Amoretto Sour, I felt someone gently grab my arm, so I turned my head and laid my eyes on the sexiest tall, bald headed, chocolate brother I had ever seen in my life. He leaned in closer to me and asked me in my ear if I wanted to dance with him. I took his hand and led him to the dance floor. 'Ol boy didn't have rhythm to save his life, but where he lacked in the rhythm department he definitely made up for in the looks department.

Qamar

As soon as I got in front of the club I texted Talisha to ask her where she was. She replied that she was posted at the bar near the patio, so I made my way over there.

"Yo, where is Qortni? Have you seen her since you messaged me?"

"Yeah, she's over there on the dance floor, not too far from the first bar."

"Aight, I'll be right back, I'm about to fuck this bitch up."

"Handle ya b.i. playa," Talisha responded with a smirk on her face.

Qortni had her back towards the bar I was coming from so she didn't even notice me approaching her.

"So you couldn't respond to any of my calls or messages but you can bring your ass out to a club and have a host of dudes around you like you're single?" I asked her in her ear so she could hear me over the noisy club music.

"Who the fuck are you talking to like you own me? Mothafuckas must really not know who the fuck I am, but they are definitely about to find out."

When Qortni turned around, my whole face dropped 'cause I was standing in front of Amberlin, Qortni's cousin who looks exactly like her.

"Yo Amberlin, my bad ma, my homegirl shot me a message and told me Qortni was down here and being that she hadn't hit my jack back after I called and texted her, I figured I'd come down here and check her."

Instead of responding to me, she hit me with a two-piece, once in my jewels and one dead in my face. I can't even front she definitely caught me totally off guard, I know I approached her, but it was only because I thought she was Qortni, but I didn't think me approaching her like that would give her reason enough for her to two-piece me like that.

18

"That shit right there is for your punk ass putting your hands on my cousin, she wouldn't hit you back, but rest assured I pack enough animosity for the both of us, you bitch ass."

Real talk, I couldn't even be mad at shorty for hitting me, but I was damn sure tight 'cause she laid me out in front of everyone, strangers, people I know, shit even some of my closest friends.

A s I was finishing up what I had started in my journal I noticed my cousin was blowing my phone up, so I hit her back immediately.

"What's up chica? Everything straight?"

"Bitch, you won't believe what the fuck just happened in the club."

"Spill it!! I need some excitement in my life right about now!"

"I'm on my way to your crib now, come outside now."

I got dressed and as soon as I opened my front door my cousin was just then pulling up, as soon I hopped in her car my phone started singing Aaliyah's At Your Best, it was Qamar calling me.

"Can I help you?" I asked agitated.

"Yo, come outside in fifteen minutes, I need to holla at you and it can't wait until tomorrow."

"I'm outside already, I'm about to talk to my cousin."

"Tell her to hit the bricks; I need your undivided attention."

"Well, it'll have to wait until tomorrow 'cause my family comes first Q."

"Listen to me, if you're not done talking to her by the time I get there then I'm done with you, real shit."

"Well, I'll see ya when I see ya," I told him right before hanging up on him, and turning my phone off.

"Was that punk ass Qamar?"

"Yeah, but I'm not going there about him right now, tell me what the hell happened in the club tonight?" I asked her 'cause the suspense of what she wanted to tell me was irking me to no good.

Just as Amber was about to tell me what happened her phone began ringing.

"What's up papí?" She answered her phone.

"You heard exactly what the hell I said, I have thought about it, I didn't stutter the first time I told you, I want that dude to know he

20

fucked up royally, he needs to feel my wrath, and I need for you to make that happen," she told whomever was on the phone.

I was officially lost, but what ever happened in the club must have been serious, 'cause Amber never calls up her goon squad unless it's something major.

"Um, ok I'm officially lost, what the hell happened in the club that has you calling ya whole goon squad up? Which one of your boo thangs got it fucked up with you tonight?"

"Why did Qamar roll up on me in the club tonight thinking I was you and start popping off at the mouth before he realized I wasn't you?"

"Wait, how did he figure you were me? Why would he think I was in the club?"

"Hell if I know, but he was damn sure coming out of pocket so I decided to do what I felt was the best thing for me to do and I two-pieced him right in the club in front of everyone."

"You did not!"

"Yes the hell I did and my swollen fists right here are my witnesses," she said holding up her very noticeably swollen fists.

"You want to come in the crib to put some ice on them? They look like they're swelling by the second, not a good look."

"Nah I'm good, but let me ask you something and I want you to tell me the truth, the God's honest truth, no bullshit."

"Ask away."

"Why do you put up with Qamar's bullshit? Don't you realize you're worth so much more than what you're going through with him? Has he hit you before?"

I knew this series of questions was coming but I didn't expect them to come this soon. Since we were younger Amberlin has always been extra overprotective of me, even though I'm the older of the two of us.

"Honestly? I'm scared that if I try to leave him, he'll try to kill me, him and I fit well together, very compatible as long as I don't do anything or say anything to piss him off. I don't have to worry about him hitting me or anything like that. This is the first and last time he's put his hands on me, I promise you that, he won't do it again," I told her trying to convince myself of that more than her.

T his chick is really not answering her phone now? I said aloud to myself.

I didn't think Qortni was going to take my statement 'bout me being good on her if she didn't meet me outside instead of talking to her cousin, but she did and now she's not answering any of my calls or messages, for the second time tonight. I thought about just dropping by her crib but I thought better of it 'cause I really didn't know her frame of mind after today's events.

Since I couldn't get in touch with Qortni, I decided to give Talisha a call since she was partly to blame for me getting chumped in the club by Amberlin.

"Yo Q, you good my dude?"

"Kill all that concerned bullshit aight? You're partly to blame for me getting my ass handed to me tonight, got me spazzing out on a shorty who wasn't even my shorty, now my girl doesn't want to have shit to do with me."

"Damn my guy, stop crying over some bitch that doesn't give two flyin' fucks about you. How the hell was I supposed to know that trick has a twin sister around here? I don't associate with her, I don't be around her. I was just trying to be of some assistance since the chick in the club, who I thought was ya girl had a bunch of guys around her, as your friend, I took that as being disrespectful."

"I don't recall telling you to come to the club and make an ass out of yourself, so don't try to blame me for 'ole girl knocking you on your ass in front of everyone, that's all your fault playa," Talisha told me holding nothing back.

"I never said it was all your fault, but shit, you've been around my girl enough times to know what the fuck she looks like, how the fuck were you not able to tell that wasn't her? You know what? Never mind, what's done is done, I gotta figure out a way to get my girl back. I'm off this." I told her without giving her the chance to reply.

Being that Qort wasn't answering my calls or messages I decided to ride by her crib to see if by chance she was still outside talking to her cousin, even though Amberlin was the last person I was trying to run into. When I got to the light right before Qortni's house I noticed Amber's truck parked in front and the two of them sitting outside; I decided to not press my luck and roll up on them, cause with the luck I was having recently they'd both mess around and jump on me, and I wasn't trying to have that happen. I decided to just keep driving until I wound up back at my crib, I would have to go see her tomorrow.

"Wait, I know he didn't just ride by to see if I had another guy over here with me since I haven't retuned any of his calls or messages."

"That was him that just rode by?"

"Yeah."

"You want to go by his house so we can beat the brakes off his bitch ass?"

"Nah he's not worth all of that."

"So, what are you going to do as far as your relationship with him? I mean do you think he really won't put his hands on you again?"

"Honestly, I would love to believe he won't but with him, there's just no telling, I think anything is possible with him. Do I love him, no, he's basically just something for me to do, someone to roll with me to dinner or the movies. I sometimes wish him and I never met and never linked up, I feel as if I'd be a lot better off without him."

"So, why won't you stick to your guns and really be done with him? I mean really Qortni, you're a beautiful woman, you have a lot going for yourself, you're holding down two jobs, you have your own whip, you need to stop bullshitting and get your writing going cause you have mega talent with a pen and paper. Personally, I think you can do a lot better than him, but then again that's just my opinion."

"I hear you cuz, and I agree with you but it's easier said than done to just leave him, like my emotions right now are so all over the place, between your aunt not liking me and making me aware that she's not happy with the fact that she birthed me, him and his bitch fits, I'm just so over everyone right now. I don't know whether I'm coming or going half of the time, don't know which way is up or which way is down."

"Well, you know no matter what, I have your back with whatever decision you make. Have you two thought about counseling? Just to help sort through problems and to have a neutral party hear you out and give suggestions to help you?"

"I had mentioned to him not to long ago about going to see a relationship therapist, but he wasn't trying to hear it, then I mentioned to him about taking some time off, which is what I really think we need and he was against that too, he said that would just allow me more time to meet other guys and link up with them. Amber, I don't know what the hell I'm going to do, I swear I don't," I told her and banged my fist into my hand.

"Like I just told you Qort, whatever you decide, I'm going to have your back, I'm very concerned about your well being and I want what's best for you because you deserve nothing but the best. We may be first cousins but we've always acted and treated each other as if we were sisters, you know I'm only a phone call away whenever you need anything," Amberlin told me while embracing me in a hug.

Amber and I talked about miscellaneous things for about half an hour more until she got a call from her flavor of the month, she told me she wanted to do breakfast in the morning and we promised to touch bases with one another once we each got up and situated.

When I finally got back to my room I turned my phone back on and put it on the charger, once it received all of the messages, I noticed Qamar had sent me like twenty text messages, most of them I skimmed through and deleted, and the last six that were in my inbox all went together, and like a dummy I sat and read them.

The series of messages that all went together read, "Shorty, I know I'm probably the last person you want to see or hear from but I need to let you know something, first off, I never meant to put my hands on you the earlier today, that happened straight out of emotions and anger, I promise to you from the bottom of my heart I will NEVER put my hands on you again. You are my future, my life, my world, and I don't want to lose you due to my stupidity or my temper. I love you with my entire soul Baby and I can't see myself being with anyone else for the rest of my life but you. I don't expect a response from you tonight or even tomorrow, I just wanted to apologize for the shit I put you through and wanted to let you know that I really didn't mean what I said about you either coming outside to talk to me and leave your cousin behind or I was good on you. All of that was said out of anger, not towards you but just on the strength of your cousin making me look like a fool in front of everyone in the club. I guess I've said all I've needed or wanted to say. So think about it and hit me whenever you're ready to talk. Love you forever and a day. ~ Q."

I can't even lie; those messages touched a part of my heart that I really didn't want touched. Instead of texting him back, I turned my phone off, turned my R&B playlist on my iPod, hit the lights in my room, laid across my bed and allowed my thoughts to run wild until I fell asleep.

Amberlin

I swear love my cousin but sometimes she makes the absolute worse decisions when it comes to men. I couldn't help myself when I saw Qamar's punk ass in the club tonight. I think it was best that Qortni didn't come out with me 'cause there's no doubt in my mind that we both would have ended up in jail tonight and neither of us would have been able to see the judge until Monday. I should have listened to the little voice in my head that was telling me to play the crib tonight, but me being me; I didn't listen. What I'm still trying to figure out is who in the hell could have mistaken me for my cousin and told Qamar that Qort was in the club? Now my investigation begins and God so help the person it was 'cause I'm definitely going to knock someone's ass out once I find out. One thing I know is that it was a female, because no guy is going to tell his boy that his wifey is at the club dancing with another dude, that's some straight hating ass bitch type shit.

Qortni is probably going to kick my ass for texting her so late, but I need to know whom she's beefing with and if she knows where the bitch lives

"Qort, don't beat my ass for texting you so late even though I just left your crib, but I've been doing some thinking about the events at the club tonight, and I've come to the conclusion that it had to be a female that told Qamar that you were here. I need to know who you're beefing with, why you chose not to tell me you have beef and if you know where that bitch or those bitches live, if it's more than one that you're beefing with. Hit me back ASAP!"

I waited for a response for her for about ten minutes, and when I didn't get one, I decided to call her, but no such luck; her phone went straight to voicemail. I guess she had a more exhausting day than I thought. Guess I'll just have to wait until she and I go to breakfast to hit her with more questions. I need to get some sleep if I plan on going anywhere in the morning.

S itting here in my room I've had time to really think about the events of yesterday and earlier today at the club, and as much as I hate admitting it, I fucked up big time, and hopefully I can get Qortni to at least hear me out or talk to me because I can't see myself with anyone else but her. I can't see myself having children with anyone but her; she is my future wife, the mother of my future children, my life and my world. I didn't mean to send her such a long text message, mainly because I know shit like that is one of her pet peeves, but the things I put in that message are the things I wouldn't be able to say to her face to face or even over the phone, all because of my super high ego. Call me a bitch because I'm texting my emotions to my girl; it is what it is. I'd like to see how many men could honestly say they would sit their woman down and tell them what they're feeling, and actually do it.

Qortni didn't respond to my message so I'm assuming one of two things happened; one, she either has her phone off or two; she read the message and just decided not to respond to it. Whichever happened, I can't even be mad at her cause I'm the one that fucked up royally.

As I was dozing off to sleep my phone alerted me that I had a new text message, I only picked up my phone to look at it 'cause I thought it might have been Qortni, but it wasn't, it was Talisha, one of the last people I wanted to hear from right about now. I started to ignore her, but I said fuck it 'cause I wanted to see what she had to say, I didn't want to chance her driving to my crib and causing a scene.

Her first message read, "Yo, what's good, you up?"

"Yeah, what do you want?"

"Just wanted to make sure you were good and we were straight with one another."

"Honestly Tee, I'm not really feeling you right now. I think there are some feelings on your end towards me that are deeper than just a friendship and if in fact that is true, we need to separate this friendship

29

for a while, 'cause our friendship may have caused me to lose my future wife."

"Really Q? Your bitch must have put that dumb shit in your head; you know we've been friends since we were in diapers. You really think I have feelings towards you that I'm not telling you about? My answer to that is hell no I don't have feelings for you that go beyond a friendship, but I will say this, and it may sound crazy, but I do agree with you on one thing, we definitely need to take a breather from one another, cause obviously you can't tell who is in your corner and who is fucking against you. Don't bother texting me back cause all of your messages will go unanswered, deuces."

I didn't even bother responding to her after that, there was really no point in it, but she did leave me wondering if I had made yet another mistake by thinking that Talisha had romantic feelings for me; then again I thought about something, Talisha never gets mad over things unless there's some type of truth to them, which only confirmed that I was right. After my conversation with Talisha, I really felt like shit for telling Qortni that she was delusional for thinking that Talisha had feelings for me, and for telling her that she was only trying to tell me that 'cause she was trying to cover up some shit on her end.

That conversation with Talisha and all the other events of the day really started to make my head hurt, I need to get some sleep and try to figure out how I'm going to make things right with Qortni and I'm definitely going have to pray to God that Qortni finds it in her heart to forgive me so we can move our relationship forward and put all of this shit behind us.

I wasn't able to sleep for shit last night, between my thoughts running wild and countless nightmares waking me, I'm a freaking mess this morning and I honestly don't feel like going to breakfast with Amber If I try to back out, she won't let me hear the end of it, so I guess I need to get my ass up and get ready.

I decided not to turn my phone on until after I get out of the shower cause I know I have messages that I'm not going to want to read, especially from Qamar. Speaking of him, my mind is still trying to digest the message he sent me last night I wish I believed the shit he said in his message but I just don't. I want to text him and tell him that we just need to let each other be and if it's meant to be between us it'll be somewhere down the line; matter of fact, I'm going to text him while Amber and I are out today.

When I got downstairs to the second floor to take my shower, my mother tried to start up a conversation with me.

"You look like you didn't sleep too well last night."

"I didn't," I replied to my mother not really in the mood to talk to her this morning.

"Is everything all right?"

"Yup," I replied rolling my eyes.

I made my way to the bathroom and purposely locked the door just in case she tried to come in and play twenty-one questions with me while I was in the shower. After I got out of the shower I called Amber to see what time she wanted to link up.

"Hey hoe, what time do you want to link up for breakfast or brunch?"

"How about in half an hour? Or do you need more time than that?"

"Nah, that's cool, I just got out of the shower, so all I have to do now is get dressed. Are we riding together or driving separately?"

"I'm coming to pick you up, 'cause after we eat, we are going shopping. Oh, before I forget to ask you, did you get my text that I sent you earlier this morning?"

"No, I haven't looked through my messages yet, what's up?"

"Nothing, we'll talk when I pick you up."

"See ya in a little while."

No sooner than I got off the phone with Amber, my phone began signing Lovers and Friends By Lil Jon, alerting me that Qamar was calling me.

"Hey Q."

"Hey babe, how come you sound like you don't want to be on the phone with me? Are you busy?"

"I sound like that because I really don't want to be bothered by you now, and yes, I am busy, I'm on my way out."

"Where are you off to and who are you going with?"

"I don't think that's any of your business remember, we broke up last night?"

"Yeah, that's why I called you, we need to talk."

" I agree, but not right now, I'll hit you up later when I have some free time."

"Okay, fair enough, but I must tell you that I really think you're going to be surprised with what I have to tell you."

"As I'm sure you're going to be blown away with what I have to say to you."

"Well, I won't hold you since you said you're busy, just hit my hip when you're available to talk."

"Yup," I replied and hung up.

After hanging up with Q, I heard my cousin's horn beeping alerting me that she was outside, so I grabbed my bag, and made my way out the door.

"Hey hoe, you look like shit, didn't sleep well last night?" Amberlin greeted me as soon as I got in her truck.

"Not in the least bit, I think I'm going to tell Qamar that we really need some time apart; he got mad at me last night 'cause we were out here talking and I wouldn't tell you to bounce so he and I could talk. He had the audacity to tell me to tell you to hit the bricks, and when I told him family came first, he called himself giving me the ultimatum either I tell you to leave so he and I could talk or he was going to be good on me, and well, you know the rest."

"How many times has he called and texted you? He's really stuck on himself isn't he?"

"I can't even remember how many text messages and calls I've gotten from him; I know it's too damn many. Most of the messages that came through my phone from him I deleted without even reading. I just got off the phone with him right before I came out here to meet you, he supposedly has some great news to tell me, but I'm not even trying to hear it, I need some time away from him," I responded to my cousin while rubbing the temples of my head.

"Let me ask you this, 'cause something kept irking me last night after I left your house, are you beefing with anyone? Are any of his home girls beefing with you and you haven't told me?"

"I'm not beefin' with anyone to my knowledge, but you know how chicks are, they can be beefin' with you hard body and you can be totally oblivious to it, and as far as his home girls, only one of them to my knowledge can't stand me, and the feelings are mutual on my end. This chick Talisha, they supposedly grew up together, she lives up the street from him, he says there aren't any romantic feelings from either one to the other, but I'm not buying that bullshit; why do you ask?"

"I've been trying to figure something out since the club incident. Now, I don't know about you but I'm thinking the person that contacted Qamar and told him you were in the club last night was a female, 'cause only some bitch who's trying to start some shit between a female and her man will do some shady shit like that, no guys that I know will do some shit like that. I know the guys Qamar rocks with, not one of them would do that; for him to know exactly where I was standing, being around a bunch of guys on the dance floor...

I cut her off in mid sentence, "I can bet you any amount of money it was that bitch Talisha. I always told Qamar that her feelings for him go way beyond being just friends, but he always acts like he doesn't see it, and he denies it, but now that you said something, it has her name written all over it. She figured if she told him I was at the club with a bunch of guys around me, he'd come down there, dumb out on me and she'd be there to help him take his mind off of everything after all was said and done."

"Exactly," Amberlin said.

"The nerve of that slut."

"The nerve of them both."

I began laughing out of nowhere, and Amberlin was looking at me like I was crazy.

"What the hell is so funny?" She asked with the most perplexed look on her face.

"I'm just now putting the pieces together. He called me right after we hung up this morning telling me that we needed to talk and that I was going to be very surprised with what he needed to tell me. I will bet you any amount of money that he is going to tell me that he and Talisha are no longer friends..."

"And that he wants to make things between the both of you work," Amber stated finishing my thought.

The she said, "I know he probably hates the fact that you grew up with a bunch of men 'cause you can see shit before it happens; you really thinks he's going to tell you he wants to make it work between the two of you?"

"I know for a fact that's what he's going to tell me but I don't even want to be bothered with him anymore for now, I just want to do me and enjoy life."

"Well, on our way back from the mall, I want you to show me where that bitch lives, she and I have an appointment with one another and she doesn't even know it yet. What are you going to do about you and Qamar?"

"No, Amber, let that bitch be, karma will get her and him, I don't want you getting into any type of trouble 'cause of me. I really don't even want to meet up with him later to talk to him, I just want to be able to let my hair down for a while, and not have to worry about thirsty chicks clocking my every move, or calling and texting him whenever I make a move."

"I feel you girl; okay, let's switch the topic, I'm starting to get a headache from all of this and this ain't even my situation. I have a great idea to get both of our minds off of your situation, how about we go out tonight? Celebrate your new found single life, you down?"

"Hell yeah I'm down, just curious, what stores are we hitting up and are we eating first or shopping, 'cause this sister right here is past hungry."

"Nah, you're not past hungry, ya ass is just greedy, don't think I didn't notice that you've been gaining weight, let me find out you're pregnant."

I replied to her while we made our way to the mall food court, "Hell no, well, let me rephrase that, I don't think so, but I did notice I have been gaining weight, I pray to God I'm not pregnant, I can't stomach having to deal with Qamar for eighteen years as my child's father, the mere thought of it gives me chills."

After ordering our food, Amberlin tilted her head to the side, looked at me and said, "Did you just hear what you said? If you can't imagine having children with him, then why the hell would you want to be in a relationship with him?"

"I'm just having fun, I'm too young to be thinking 'bout kids or being in a serious relationship, so let's just drop it please?"

After we ate we hit the stores in the mall to find an outfit for the club tonight and I think in the three hours we were in the mall, we both spent about fifteen hundred dollars and Qamar must have called my phone at least ten times, and he was really starting to get on my last damn nerve. Once Amberlin and I got back into her truck I decided to call Qamar back and see why he had been blowing my phone up the way he had been.

On the first ring he answered, "Hey Qort, I thought you had forgotten about me, are you still available today to talk to me?"

"How could I possibly forget about you with you calling my phone every fifteen minutes? I'm on my way home now, so when I get home and get settled, I'll give you a call so we can meet and talk."

"I apologize if I've been being a pain in the ass to you today, I just have a lot to tell you and I really think you're going to be very pleased with what I have to tell you."

"Well, we'll see about that in about an hour or so Q, bye." I told him and hanging up before he had the opportunity to respond.

As soon as I hung up the phone with Qamar, Amber asked me, "Girl, why in the hell is he so annoying? Has he always been like this?"

"Hell yeah he's always been like this, and I can't stand it, but how come I never realized, until now, how annoying his ass is?"

"You haven't ever noticed how annoying his ass was 'cause your 'love' for him wouldn't allow you to see it," Amber replied making air quotations around the word love.

My cousin and I both knew that deep down inside I didn't love Qamar, I was with him because he was something to do, we kind of fit well together and everyone around us wanted us to work; it was one of those situations where I was hoping that as time went by I would begin to love him.

Qamar tells me all of the time that he loves me, and I honestly believe him, I like to describe his love for me as the type of love Mary J. Blige and Method Man talked about in her song *Real Love*. I think if he and I take this much needed break from one another for about a month or so and we get back together, there's no doubt in my mind that our relationship will be better and stronger and we'll be able to move forward and possibly be together for the long run.

"You're absolutely right," I responded to Amberlin's statement.

When we got in front of my house, I told Amber that I was going to call her once I finished talking to Qamar and that I was going to shower and get dressed at her house tonight; I unloaded all of my bags from her trunk, got in my car and called Qamar.

"Hey, where did you want me to meet you at? Your crib is not an option," I asked as soon as he answered the phone.

If you want to get something to eat we can go to Chili's on Dixwell Ave. or we can meet at East Rock."

"I've already eaten so we can meet in the parking lot of East Rock. How long is it going to take you to get there?" I was not about to go to the top of East Rock Mountain with this fool so he could try to throw me off after I tell him what I need to tell him.

"I'm around that area now so it's only going to take me about a minute or so to get there, how about you?"

"I'll be there in about five minutes, see ya when I get there," I responded to him then hung up.

I don't know what's been up with my attitude lately but I've been real bitchy and my patience level has been shorter than short, something has got to give. Once I got to East Rock I got out of my car and sat on the trunk. He got out and stood by the back of his whip, the look on his face told me that he was waiting for me to come over to where he was at, but he must have looked at my face, 'cause my face damn sure told him I wasn't moving, so if he wanted to be closer to me he'd better come over to my car, which he did.

As soon as Qamar got within two feet next to me, I couldn't fight the urge in me, I punched Qamar dead in his face, and I know I caught him off guard.

"Qortni, what the fuck did you do that for?"

"Do you really have to ask? I felt the urge to give your ass a taste of the bullshit you've been putting me through, giving you a taste of your own medicine, how do you like it?"

"I have to admit you hit like a man, but I see now why you did it, which is one of the reasons I asked you to meet me so we can talk. First and foremost I want to apologize for all the shit I've put you through, and I wanted to tell you that you were right the whole time about Talisha and her true feelings towards me. So last night, I dismissed her out of my life, so now hopefully we can move forward now that's she's a non factor, so do you think we can move forward with our relationship?"

I'm shocked that you actually admitted that I was right about her, but on the flip side of things, we really need to take a break from one another, like a month or so just so we can get things situated with ourselves; like honestly, I don't see us moving forward unless we take this break. We've been spending every waking moment with one another since we made it official and we haven't given each other much breathing space, space every relationship needs. If we're not laid up under one another, we're on the phone or texting one another, no type of breathing space."

As soon as Qamar was about to respond, I began throwing up everything I had ate for lunch, I don't know what was going on with me, but I damn sure wasn't liking it, something has to give and quickly.

"Qort, are you alright?"

"Yeah, I'm good, now what were you about to say?

Qamar began laughing and I wasn't too sure as to what was so funny.

"What are you laughing at?"

"You, how do you go from puking your brains out to asking me what I was about to say? Are you sure you're alright?"

"Because I'm me, yes I'm fine, now what were you about to say?"

"I had a feeling all you said was going to be said today, but I can't even knock you for it, I have not one to blame but myself for this shit, I'm not even going to fight or argue with you about it cause I know that'll make things a lot worse and that's the last thing I want to do to you or even us. I just have one question for you though, being that we're giving each other space now, does that mean we're allowed to sleep with other people?"

Typical guy for you always worried about getting his dick wet and at the craziest times too, I had to stifle a laugh, and this dude is crazy. "Yes, if you'd like to fuck other chicks, then be my guest Qamar."

"Aight Qort, I guess we'll keep in touch from time to time from now on."

"Yes, I guess we'll be seeing each other around, I replied to him, embracing him in a hug for the road so to speak.

Once I got back in my car I took my phone out to call Amber to let her know that I was on my way over to her house, and as soon as I hung up, Qamar was tapping on my window, so I started my car to let the window down.

"Everything alright Q?"

"Yes, I was just wondering if it was possible for us to fuck one more time before we officially go on break from one another?"

How did I know that was coming? I looked at him for a few seconds and responded, "how about I call you after I leave the club tonight and if you decide to answer we can make moves from there."

"Aight, that's a good enough answer for me, I'll be waiting on your call," he told me, then leaned in and kissed me on my forehead.

Qamar

After the events of the past couple of days or so, I already kind of knew where Qortni's head was concerning our relationship. I wasn't too surprised at her wanting to take a break, but I was surprised that she didn't give too much attention to the fact that I finally admitted that she was right about Talisha's feelings towards me and how I dismissed her from my circle so she and I could focus on our relationship and not have to worry about anyone hating or throwing salt on us. Qortni didn't even mention the text message I sent her after her cousin made a damn fool of me in the club, I mean I really poured his heart out in those messages, and for her not to even mention it, had me kind of vexed, but what can I do about that shit now? Absolutely nothing.

Since I'm a newly single man I decided to call Nate and Nature to see what they were getting into tonight 'cause I definitely wasn't trying to stay in the house and have thoughts of Qortni running through my mind. So I hit Nathan up and told him to get Nature on three-way.

"Everyone on deck?" Nate asked.

"Yeah, we all here, what's popping tonight?" I replied.

"Shit, trying to find something to get into tonight, not trying to stay in the crib."

"That's why I was hitting y'all up, Qortni and I separated today and I'm not trying to stay in the crib and drive myself crazy, so where are we going tonight? I'm not trying to go anywhere where everyone is going to be at, I'm trying to go somewhere low-key but that's still popping."

"Say word y'all broke up? What the fuck happened?" Nature asked.

"Talisha had hit my jack the other night with a text that said that Qortni was in the club with a bunch of dudes around her, so I went down there and approached her only to find out that it was her cousin Amberlin, not her."

"That's the only reason y'all broke up? Doesn't sound like a valid enough reason to me for y'all to just separate like that," my cousin Nate asked.

"Nah, that's not the only reason we split, as y'all know I have a bad temper, and sometimes I let my temper get the best of me, and I may hit her, like the other day y'all was here and was playing twenty-one questions with her, I got beside myself and punched her in the fuckin' face; it's a whole lot of shit going on and we just need some time to ourselves."

"Yo, on some real shit, have you ever thought about anger management classes? Maybe you should think about checking them out, I had to take them after I had that last incident with shorty," Nature asked.

"Qortni mentioned to me about going to counseling but I shot it down, not really feeling the whole idea of telling a bunch of strangers my personal problems. I'll just have to find something to do to channel my negative energy when I get pissed off, I can't go too much time without my baby girl, and Qort is my life.

"Aight, enough of the Lifetime drama and love shit, where are we going tonight? Please don't say Van Dome cause I'll stay the fuck home before I go there," Nature said.

"I don't know homie, Van Dome is having their freakum dress party tonight, you know there are going to be some bad chicks in there tonight, I think that may be the move we need to make tonight," Nate replied to Nature.

"I think I'm with Nature on this one, I think Van Dome is a bad choice, how about we hit up the Cat Walk, I'm in the mood to see some bad bitches, big titties and throw dollars on them to see them make their asses clap," I told them both.

"Okay, the Cat Walk it is, what time are we heading over there, and are we riding together or meeting up there?"

"Eleven o'clock should be a good enough time to head over there, but yo, I got bottles over here at the crib, I want to drink before we head over there, y'all trying to drink?" I asked the both of them.

"Hell yeah we drinking, we can meet you at your crib by ten, pop them bottles, and then head over to the club," Nature replied.

After we downed two bottles of Hennessey, and a bottle of Hypnotiq we made our way to the Cat Walk and we were totally disappointed, there were some slack ass looking strippers in that club, bunch of out of shape, not worth a damn penny type of bitches in there, as soon as we got there turned right back around and left.

"So being that the Cat Walk is out of the question for tonight, where are we headed now? I'm not trying to go home and blow my buzz," I asked the guys.

"Only other option around here tonight is the Van Dome, none of us are sober enough to drive to Hartford," Nature replied.

"Van Dome it is then, I mean we can't go wrong, freakum dress night, bunch of New Haven's finest up in there with hardly nothing on, I know I'm in there," Nate replied.

I really wasn't in the mood to be at the Dome tonight, but I was outnumbered, two to one, so I had to suck it up and just go with the flow, I was not about to hear these two getting on me because I was complaining about going to that particular club.

A mber and I both showered and got dressed at her crib and did our little photo session with one another and then headed to the club. Tonight was the Van Dome's annual Freakum Dress contest and even though I'm sure I wasn't going to win the contest, I was still killin' the mini BabyPhat dress I was wearing, and my cousin was rocking the hell out of the RocaWear mini she was donning.

I noticed Qamar's car in the lot while we were riding around looking for a parking space and I really didn't feel like being bothered with his ass tonight, but going to another club was not an option, so I said a quick prayer that he nor Amberlin would show their asses and we'd all just enjoy the night.

When we got in line we noticed a few regular faces, said hey and kept it moving to the front of the line, being that Amber and I knew the owner personally we went right into the club without having to pay and made a b-line to the bar. I ordered two Amoretto Sours, one for each hand, Amberlin ordered two shots of Hennessey and we made our way over to the dance floor. This fine ass tall, dark chocolate man grabbed me by my waist, which alerted me that he wanted to dance, and I damn sure didn't turn him down. As ole boy and I were dancing I felt a pair of eyes watching me and I didn't like that feeling at all, so me being the bitch I wanted to be, I decided to grind on him a lil harder and as I was dancing with him I kept subliminally looking around to see whose eyes were piercing a whole through my body, and lo and behold, it was Qamar staring at me hard from the bar near the club's patio.

As *Lights Camera Action* by Mr. Cheeks was fading out, I told Mr. Chocolate that I needed to go to the bar and re-up on my drinks, so he walked with me to the bar with his hands on my waist, ordered my drinks as well as his drink, paid for it all, then we headed back to the dance floor. Once our drinks were gone, the DJ started playing Christina Millian's *Dip It Low* and I decided to give Qamar's ass a show since he thought he was playing Mr. I Spy, I decided to give him a show he's definitely never forget. I pushed Mr. Chocolate into a chair that was near the dance floor and gave him a lap dance he'd never forget, and I know every guy in the club was sure to remember it too, especially Qamar.

After that song went off Amberlin grabbed me by my wrist and damn near dragged me to the bathroom where she cussed me out.

"Bitch, are you crazy giving that guy a lap dance knowing Qamar's psychotic ass is sitting in that damn corner clocking your every move? You know his ass is liable to start a fuckin' scene in here, we need to bounce like right now," Amber scolded me.

"No, I'm not crazy, Qamar and I are no longer together so I can give lap dances to whomever I please, if Qamar wants to start some shit in here, let him, he'll definitely regret it 'cause I have people all up in through here, let his ass bust bad, he'll end up in someone's morgue tonight fucking with me. Now you can leave if you like, but as for me, I haven't finished showing my dress off yet, so I'm staying til the lights come on and they give the last call for alcohol," I replied to her while checking my hair and makeup in the mirror.

"Have it your way mama, you know I'll be close by just in case he tries to start something 'cause you know I have no problem regulating on his ass again."

"I bet you don't," I replied to her laughing.

I continued, "Let's go back out there and try to win this contest."

"Right behind you cousin."

The rest of the night in the club went well without any bullshit from Qamar, Amberlin won the contest, I didn't even know my cousin knew how to work a stripper pole the way she did, shit more power to her 'cause she and I split her prize money, another five hundred dollars in my pocket.

As Amberlin and I were leaving the club and walking to her truck we noticed Qamar, Nate and Nature all standing around her truck, I knew he wanted to talk to me about the lap dance I gave that dude earlier, but I really wasn't trying to hear him tonight He and I aren't together any longer so technically he has no reason to get upset, but I know how he's thinking, once I'm his, I'll always be his, even if we're taking a break from one another, silly boy, bitch fits are for bitches.

Amberlin was so busy going on and on about her winning the contest she didn't realize until we were damn near at her truck that Qamar and his peoples were there. Then she asked me, "Um, so what are you going to do about Mr. Possessive over there?"

"I'm not going to do anything, we're going to get in your truck and bounce, and I have nothing to say to him."

"Suit yourself but you already know he's going to start some shit; he better pray his boys over there holds his ass back if he tries to bust a move."

We continued to walk over to Amberlin's truck and I attempted to walk over to the door to get in but Qamar's annoying ass grabbed me by my waist and asked me if him and I could talk for a minute, and of course my response was a flat out "no."

"Qortni, I just want two minutes of your time, am I asking for too much?"

"Yes you are, I'm tired, I'm ready to go home, shower and go to bed, now can you please get off of me so I can be on my merry way?"

Instead of letting my waist go, he grabbed me tighter, and that's when I lost it, instead of taking the chance of punching him in his face I did the only other thing I could do to get his hands off of me, I kneed him in his jewels, as small as they were, and he doubled over in pain; his boys burst out laughing.

"Qortni, what the fuck did you do that for? That wasn't even necessary!"

"I asked you to get off of me, you didn't so therefore I had to get you off of me the best way I knew how, now you have a good evening Qamar," I told him making my way back over to Amberlin's truck and right before I got in the car good, Qamar pulled me to the ground by my hair. Amber, Nate and Nature all came over trying to get Qamar off of me, he was officially about to go meet his maker, this idiot just didn't learn that putting his hands on me was detrimental to his health.

"Q man, what the fuck is your problem doing shit like that to Qortni? I see why she broke up with your ass; you have no type of fucking self-control! You are bugged out, and you need some serious help," Nature told Qamar.

Amberlin was pissed, I saw it all over her face, and she had been itching for Qamar to fuck up tonight, and that's exactly what he did. So Amberlin being Amberlin couldn't leave well enough alone so she went and gave Qamar a piece of her mind, plus a lil something extra.

"Qamar, I'm not going to even beat around the bush with you, you know I don't like you, never have and probably never will, you're a bitch boy just on the strength of you having no problem putting your hands on females, especially my cousin. All of these weak minded chicks around here may not mind you hitting them or choking them up, but I know my cousin has a big problem with it and I have an even bigger problem with it. Now, you know I already laid your ass out one time already when you rolled up on me in the same club not to long along when you thought I was my cousin, now you have the audacity to pull my cousin out of my vehicle by her hair? You must have fallen and bumped your head, now this is the absolute last time I want to have to talk to you about your bitch ass putting your hands on my cousin," Amberlin told him right before hitting him with a mean left hook to his face.

Nate and Nature both looked at each other, then over at Amberlin and I and quietly helped Qamar over to his car so they could all leave, I guess they said to hell with helping Qamar, he was fending for himself with this battle. I'm happy that all three of them, Amberlin, Nate and Nature all got to see first hand what Qamar put me through when he and I were together.

"Qort, are you all right? Do you want to stop anywhere to get something? I can't believe he did that, like he really had the audacity to pull you out of my car by your hair, I bet his punk ass didn't expect you or me to do anything about it, he got us both fucked up."

"I'm good cuz, I am hungry though, we can go to a diner to get something to eat, I'm staying over at your house tonight, I don't want to go home and chance having Qamar being there when I pull up, thankfully he doesn't know where you live so I don't have to worry about him stalking your place looking for me."

"You just had an altercation with your ex and all your fat ass can do is think about food? Only you, which diner to you want to go to?"

"I'm starving, feeling like I haven't eaten all day, and you and I both know that's not the case, but any diner except for that spot in West Haven is fine, I also need to stop at a drug store after we leave the diner, I think I need a pregnancy test."

"How late are you? It could just be that you're super stressed that's causing you to feel the way you've been feeling."

"I'm two weeks late, I'm never this late, even when I am stressed I'm never this late, I think I'm really pregnant," I replied with tears welling in my eyes.

"We'll stop there right after we leave the diner, I can't believe you're about to be a mommy! I'm about to be a Godmother! You already know I'm going to spoil the hell out of that baby! How do you think Qamar is going to feel about being a father?"

"First of all, calm down, we don't know for sure if I am pregnant and who said you were going to be the Godmother? Lastly, if I am pregnant, I don't think I'm going to keep it and I don't see any point in telling him I am if I am."

"You know our family doesn't believe in abortions and I know you don't either, but whatever floats your boat, and do you think it's right not to tell Qamar? I mean even though y'all are not together now what if he wants you to keep the baby? What if he wants to raise the baby? Have you thought of things from his point of view?"

Amber had a point and she was making me rethink this whole situation if I really was pregnant. I didn't think this thing all the way through from both sides, Qamar's and mine.

After we ate we headed to the drug store to get a couple of different pregnancy tests before we headed back to Amberlin's house. Once we got to her house I took one of the tests and indeed I was pregnant; after crying for about a good hour I reluctantly texted Qamar and told him we needed to talk ASAP. Being that he didn't know where Amberlin lived, I had no choice but to meet him at my house. I told Amberlin after he and I talked I'd be back over to her house.

Qamar

Qortni had officially pissed me off to the max and I know she was doing that shit on purpose. I knew she knew it was me eyeing her every move in the club, and I know she felt my eyes on her the whole time she was dancing with that clown. Even though she and I aren't together at the moment, she is still my woman, and dancing with another guy and giving complete strangers lap dances in a club where the both of us know damn near everyone in there is a slap in my face, the ultimate disrespect. I have people coming up to me asking me what the hell is wrong with Qortni, and why she is disrespecting our relationship the way she was, that shit is embarrassing,

After the club let out I took a chance with speaking to Qortni about what she was doing in the club and I think I went about it the wrong way, but Qortni is so stubborn and hard headed, she wasn't trying to hear me, so I grabbed her, and again, I let my emotions get the best of me and I had to pay the price. I don't know what was worse Qortni kneeing me in my balls or Amberlin punching me in my face, either way I guess I got what I deserved.

After Nate, Nature and I left after Amber and Qort pulled off, we decided to hit up a diner. After we ordered our food, we began talking about the events of the night.

"Yo, you just don't learn do you? You are begging for Qortni to call her goon squad and have them fuck you up," Nature directed towards me.

"I know man, I just wanted to talk to her, but she wasn't trying to hear me, can you blame me?"

After we ate and dropped Nate off I dropped Nature off to his shorty's crib and I went home and showered. After getting out of the shower I turned on my Nintendo 64 and started playing 007 and as soon as I was really getting into the game, my phone started singing to me. It was Qortni texting me, she said that she and I needed to talk ASAP. I was beginning to get a little worried 'cause whenever she told me we needed to talk ASAP the subject of conversation was never really great. I asked her if she wanted to meet me at my house or if she wanted me to meet her at her house; she chose her crib, so I made my way over there.

"So shorty, what's up? You straight disrespected me in the club tonight, fight with me after the club let out, then all of a sudden you want to talk to me about something very important. What's going on with you? What's so important?"

"So, for the past couple of weeks I've been very moody, emotional and just not feeling like myself. I have been eating like a cow, and throwing up throughout the day, I just took a home pregnancy test and found out I'm pregnant."

I was speechless for a moment; did she just tell me we are about to be parents? I don't know if I should embrace her in a hug or cuss her out for her actions tonight. I was scared and happy at the same time.

I reached in to hug her and to my surprise she didn't push me away, she hugged me back and then began weeping.

"Qort, what's the matter? Are you not happy about being pregnant?"

"I have mixed emotions about everything right now. On one hand I'm nervous about being someone's mother, but in the same breath I'm not too sure I can honestly see myself having to deal with you and your ridiculous temperament for the next twenty-one years. I don't know if I want to keep the baby or not," she told me with her tear streaked face.

"What the fuck do you mean by you don't think you can deal with me for the next twenty-one years and you're not sure if you want to keep the baby? Don't I have any say so in the matter? I am the father; I should have an opinion in the matter."

"Q, you and I both know you have a terrible temper and I'm not trying to be your human punching bag while I'm pregnant or even after I have this baby; I'm not around for the Ike and Tina type of relationship with you."

"Qort, I'm going to do whatever necessary to get help for my problem, just promise me you won't abort our baby, please, I'm begging you don't kill our baby."

"Actions speak louder than words Qamar, show me and prove to me that you are willing to change, 'cause you just saying it means absolutely nothing to me. Look, I'm getting sleepy and hungry again, I'm going to talk to you later on," she told me while heading to her car.

"Where are you going? I can go get you something to eat and bring it back here for you."

"Nah, I'm good, I'm not staying at my house tonight, I'm staying at my cousin's house, so I'm going to get my food then head back over to her place."

"How about you stay with me tonight?"

"Nah, I rather stay with my cousin tonight, she's up waiting for me; besides, she and I have some things to handle tomorrow."

"Aight shorty, have it your way, I just know you better not be lying to me about who you're staying with tonight."

She laughed and replied, "Is that a threat? That's how you get down, threatening your child's mother? Real smooth Qamar, goodnight."

Before I could even respond to her, she started her car and pulled off.

I definitely wasn't feeling the whole idea of telling Qamar that I was pregnant but I went against my own judgment and listened to Amberlin and told him. I mean why should I have told him and I wasn't even sure I was going to keep the baby? Amberlin did make a good point earlier, like the fact that our family doesn't believe in abortions, but shit, I can't stand Qamar's ass. I'm not financially ready to support myself and a child and I know my parents are going to try to kick me out once they find out. I can't knock Qamar though for wanting a say so in whether or not I keep the baby, I mean the baby is half his technically speaking, but I just honestly can't see me having to deal with him for the rest of my life. Who's to say that he'll stop acting like a bitch every time we have an argument and he won't put his hands on me any more, especially while I'm pregnant? I can't honestly say that I feel safe being pregnant around my child's father, and that's terrible. The fact that he just slightly threatened me is just a precursor as to what I would have to deal with for the next nine months or so; I'm definitely not around for that. I decided to head to the diner Amber and I left not too long ago to get something else to eat, if I keep eating like this, I will definitely be gaining major weight during the duration of this pregnancy. I called Amberlin to see if she wanted something from the diner, and after she laughed at my newfound eating habits, she told me what she wanted.

"So, how did the conversation with Qamar go? Was he excited?"

"He was overly excited, and pissed at the thought of me having an abortion, saying he should have a say in the matter."

"I mean do you blame him? He is the baby's father, and even though it is your body that will be carrying the baby, what if he wants to raise the baby?"

"I hear what the both of you are saying, I'm just not sure I want to go through nine months of my body changing, morning, noon or night sickness, or anything else that's associated with having a baby. Call me selfish, I'm calling it like I see it, I'm not ready to be a mother, I'm only nineteen years old, and you know your aunt and uncle are going to kick me out when they find out, then what the hell am I going to do; me and the baby coming to stay with you?"

"You know if you needed somewhere to stay with or without a baby my house is always open to you, I have more than enough rooms and I would also be able to help you out with the baby. All I'm asking is to not make any rash decisions, take time and think this decision through completely, pray on it mama, and know whatever decision you end up making I have your back one hundred grand."

After Amber and I finished eating and talking, I took a shower and went to bed with my thoughts racing a mile a minute.

Qamar

I couldn't believe Qortni told me that we're expecting, that was definitely not the news I was expecting to hear from her when she hit me up saying that she needed to talk to me, I thought for sure she was going to tell me that she was completely done with me. I sent messages to all of my family and my closest friends letting them know that I was about to be a father, and to start sending me their addresses so when it's time for the baby shower my family and friend's addresses will be on deck. Out of all the text messages I sent out, only two people actually called me to congratulate me and asked if it was really true, Nature and Nate.

"So, big Q is about to be a father, let me find out big homie!" Nature said.

"Hell yeah, I can't believe it my damn self. Qortni just left here not too long ago telling me the news, I'm still in shock.

"Another addition to the family, you know my mother and your mother are going to spoil that baby to no end, Qortni better get ready for that," Nathan said.

"Hell yeah, she's probably going to be mad that I done told everyone in the family already, I just couldn't contain myself though, I'm having a baby with the woman I'm going to marry."

"Here you go with that sentimental shit, man the fuck up," Nature said laughing.

"Fuck you, when you start having kids after you settle down with one female you'll see what I'm feeling, it's unexplainable."

"Whatever yo, you know what this means right? You're about to be on lockdown after the baby is born, so you might as well get all your partying and shit in now, 'cause in another eight months or so, your ass will be on lock homie!" Nature said.

"Yeah, yeah, whatever, anyhow, we all need to get up and go for drinks tomorrow to celebrate, I'm thinking maybe Friday's or Chili's for happy hour."

"That's cool with me, I gotta go, shorty is here now and we about to dip, so when you figure out the place and time hit my jack, I'll check y'all later."

After Nature hung up, I told Nathan I'd check him later, I need to lay it down for the night, busy day ahead of me, I'm going to see if Qortni will go to the baby store with me so we can start pricing things we'll need for the baby.

The Next Morning

I texted Qortni to see if she was willing to go with me to start pricing some of the big items for the baby; I was probably jumping the gun, but fuck it, it was my seed I was window shopping for. I think the time alone with Qortni would be good for the both of us, time for us to talk and see if we can work on being a couple again. It was an hour or so after I received an answer from her and she declined, she said she wasn't feeling too well, so I offered to get some things for her and bring them by her house. She declined again and said that if and when she needed something she'd either go get it herself or she'd have her cousin get it for her, which really pissed me off. I was really trying to help her out, but she was blocking me with everything I was trying to assist her with. My gut was telling me that she was with ol' boy from the club the other night, and that he was helping her during her morning sickness or whatever she was going through, so I decided to stop by her crib to see what was really up.

Qortni

I really am not in the mood for Qamar's ass today. I don't know if it's my hormones fucking with me or just his aggravating ass, but I really don't want to go window shopping for my baby when I'm not even sure if I'm keeping the damn thing, I mean really though? Who is he really trying to please? Asking me if I want to go price some items for the baby, who the hell is paying for this shit? Certainly not his no job having ass, whom was he trying to fool? I know neither one of his aunts nor his mother was going to give him money 'cause none of those old bitches really care for me and I highly doubt he told any of them that we're expecting.

I have been throwing up my insides all day since I woke up, and this lil child of mine won't let me keep anything down, not even water, and I already know if this child keeps it up, I'm going to end up in the hospital with IV's all in my arms 'cause I know I'm going to be severely dehydrated. Amberlin thought it would be best if I stayed with her while I was on my ass, so she went to my crib and picked up some of my toiletries and more clothes.

As soon as she got to my house, she called me, "Were you supposed to be meeting Qamar over here and forgot?"

"Hell no, why, he's over there?"

"Uh, yeah, staring at me from inside his car."

"What the fuck? I know he's not spying on my crib 'cause I told him I didn't want to go out with him today. This fool has officially lost his mind, his dumb ass probably thinks I didn't want to go out with him today 'cause I have someone at the crib with me, not knowing I'm not even home."

"Do you want me to go say something to him for you? You know I don't mind approaching his bitch ass."

"No, don't say anything to him, just grab my things for me and come on back here, he's not worth the headache. I'm not even in the mood to call him about why he's casing my house out like he is. I'm so over and done with him."

"All right, have it your way, I'm about to grab your things and head to get something to eat, do you want me to pick something up for you so you can try to eat?"

"I have a taste for a baked potato but I don't think anywhere around here serve just plain baked potatoes, so I'm good, I'm about to attempt to get in the shower and lay back down. I'll see you when you get back."

"Ok mamacita, I'll see you in a little while."

After hanging up with Amber, I mustered up as much strength as I could to get in the shower.

Amberlin

I feel so bad for my cousin, when I called her to see if she wanted to approach Qamar's bitch ass about him just sitting in front of her house like he was the fuckin' police she sounded so weak, that baby of hers is really kicking her ass, poor baby, she can't keep anything down, she's losing weight and she's super emotional. I pray she doesn't lose the baby, I'll be so emotional if she does, Qort is my favorite cousin, and I hate to see her going through so much right now, but I know her and I know she'll be just fine. I'm glad she decided to talk to Qamar and tell him that she was expecting, even though she claims that she doesn't know if she's keeping the baby or not, even though he is the king of assholes.

Anyhow, even though I can't stand Qamar, I respect him for wanting to go window-shopping this morning with Qort to start looking at some items for the baby, but what I want to know is who was going to pay for the shit? I hope he wasn't thinking that Qortni was coming up outta her pocket for everything they might have picked out for the baby, 'cause that shit just wasn't going to fly, but oh well, not my business so I'm not even going to get into that.

I went against my cousin's instructions and after gathering some of her clothes to bring back to my crib I went a approached this clown who had the audacity to still be sitting outside of her house like he was able to see inside of the house from where he was sitting.

"Qamar, is there any particular reason why you're sitting outside of my family's house like you're the fucking police?"

"I'm waiting on your cousin, I know she's entertaining company and that's the reason she declined going out with me earlier today to start looking at things for the baby, I'm just waiting to see the clown she has in the house with her. "

I couldn't contain myself, I laughed right in this fool's face, he was absolutely loco and he needed some serious help.

"Qamar, I'm only going to tell you this one time, so please, listen to me closely, my cousin has been in bed all damn day, the baby is putting a serious strain on her body and not allowing her to keep anything down, no food or drink, nothing, so please, miss us both with the bullshit, stop being so got damn insecure, and go home. Y'all are no longer a couple; yes you have a baby on the way with her, but damn, let her fucking live! She doesn't want to be bothered with you anymore, give her some fucking space, if she wants to be bothered by you she has your number and knows how to use it, so please, spare yourself some embarassment and stop stalking her!"

If looks could kill, I'd definitely be dead, he looked as if he wanted to fight me, but he and I both know he knew better to even try to lift one finger towards me or it would definitely be a repeat of the night he rolled up on me in the club when he thought I was Qortni.

After leaving my cousin's crib I went on a goose chase trying to find a restaurant that sold regular baked potatoes, and at last, the last restaurant I called said they did, so I ordered my food as well as Qort's and headed on home to see how she was feeling.

"Qort, I'm home and I have your baked potatoes, where are you?" I called out to her once I got in the kitchen. I didn't hear any of the televisions on but I heard the shower running, I prayed to God that she hadn't passed out in the shower, 'cause only God knows how long she's been in there. I opened the bathroom door, only to find her curled up in the fetal position, wrapped in her bathrobe sleeping.

"Qort, come on mama, let's get you into bed, you can't stay in here and sleep on the floor. How long have you been sleep on the floor?"

"I don't know, as soon as I got off the phone with you I hopped in the shower, after about ten minutes of standing, I felt myself getting nauseated and dizzy, so I slowly got out, and put my robe on. I think I need to go to the hospital; I don't want to lose the baby due to me not being able to keep anything down."

"How about you try eating a baked potato and drink some warm ginger tea; that might help, then if you can't keep any of it down, I'll take you to the hospital."

"That's fine, I can try that," she replied getting back into bed and under the covers.

I went back into the kitchen to start boiling the water for her tea and to get her baked potato for her, and I said a quick prayer that she didn't lose the baby and that whenever I decided to start having children my first trimester would be nothing compared to what Qortni is going through now, my heart goes out to her, she's a strong person and to see her so weak and down it's like I'm looking at a stranger.

Once her tea was done, I placed the potato and tea on a tray and brought it to her room for her, "Qort, your food is ready, come on so you can eat."

"I don't feel like eating, I just want to go to the hospital so they can give me something to calm my nausea, Amber, I don't want to lose my baby," she told me while rubbing her belly.

"All right mama, let's get some clothes on you so we can go to the hospital."

I swear if it weren't for my cousin, I don 't know what I'd do, she's definitely my favorite female cousin for a reason, she definitely has my back whenever I need her and vice versa.

I didn't have the strength to call Qamar and cuss him out for stalking my house the way he had been just because I didn't want to go window shopping with him for the baby, and knowing my cousin, she approached him anyway after she asked me if I wanted her to.

This is my first time being pregnant and it's not as smooth sailing as I thought it would be, this child of mine isn't allowing me to hold anything down, food nor drink, so I told Amberlin that I didn't want to try to eat anything, I just wanted to go to the hospital so the doctors could give me some type of medicine to control my nausea and vomiting every other minute.

Once we got to the hospital I got checked in and they took me right into back onto a stretcher and into a room, and I only got back so quickly because I'm pregnant.

"Don't you think you should call Qamar and let him know you're in the hospital? He may want to come here to be your support system," Amber asked me.

"I'm not calling him; I don't want him here getting on my nerves. If you don't want to stay you can leave, I'll take a cab back home, I don't mind."

"Have it your way mama, I was just suggesting it 'cause it would be a nice gesture to tell him you're here, but it is what it is, and for the record, I'm not going anywhere. I'm not leaving you here by yourself just so you can cuss me out when you're feeling better. Not going to happen cuz, so sit back, relax, and try to get some sleep while we wait for the doctor to come in and see you."

"Have it your way boss," I replied to her with sarcasm in my voice.

About twenty minutes into my nap I heard a light tap on my door and in walked my doctor.

"Hello, Ms. Monroe? My name is Dr. Jones; I understand you have been severely sick during these past few weeks with your pregnancy?"

"Nice to meet you Dr. Jones, yes I have been. I can't seem to keep anything down, no liquids, no solid foods, nothing. I'm losing weight every time I vomit, this can't be safe for me or my child. Is there anything you can give me to calm this down?"

"Losing weight in your first trimester is normal, and so is morning sickness, or as I like to call it, twenty-four seven sickness 'cause it lasts more than just in the morning. I am going to give you a prescription for a medicine called Zofran. It'll ease your nausea which will in return cut down on your vomiting and in a week or so if you see it's not getting better, call my office and we'll take action from there."

While I was talking to the doctor, I noticed that my finger must have pushed the send button on an incoming call from someone who called my phone from a blocked number, and as I asked the doctor to excuse me while I took the call, the caller hung up.

Amberlin asked the doctor, "Just curious doc, if the Zorn doesn't work for my cousin, what steps would be next to ensure she doesn't lose the baby? My biggest concern is being that she can't keep any liquids down. Won't that make her severely dehydrated, which will in return make the baby dehydrated?"

"You are indeed right, future doctor over here?" Doctor Jones replied while flirting with Amber.

"No, no doctor over here, I read a lot and I've been researching some things since my cousin has been going through with her pregnancy. I was trying to find things to help her out so she wouldn't have to be subjected to coming here today, but she insisted on coming."

"Respect, but let me run to write your prescription so you can get out of this noisy ass hospital," he responded while looking at me.

"Let me find out your new boo is going to be Dr. Jones, good thing you didn't leave huh?" I teased Amber.

"Bitch please, he isn't hardly thinking about me, he's probably dating one of the nurses around here, I'm all set."

"You and I both know he was checking for you so stop trying to play dumb and you and I both know you were checking for him too. I saw you sizing him up."

Doctor Jones came back in to the room, handed me my prescription and handed Amber a folded up piece of paper, which I'm assuming had his name and number on it.

Qamar

I really wanted to knock Amberlin's ass out for coming at me the way she did. I didn't appreciate the tone in which she used with me while I was in front of Qortni's house and the hood shit about that whole incident was the way she just walked away without me saying another word about the situation, but oh well, I'll give her that one.

All the pieces to the puzzle are starting to come together now. Qortni didn't want to go out with me because she and her cousin were busy entertaining a man, so that means I'm really going to have to whoop her ass cause she's playing games with my emotions. I don't really have the time nor the patience for her shit. No way in hell is the mother of my child going to be entertaining another man while she's carrying my seed, I'm just not having it. I can't rough her up too much 'cause she's pregnant, I'm going to do just enough to let her know I mean business.

Two Days Later

I wanted to wait a couple of days before I decided to approach Qortni about the guy she was talking to when I called her phone from a blocked number, I decided to send her a text message instead of calling 'cause I know she wouldn't have answered my call.

"Hey love, I know we haven't talked in a while, I just wanted to know if you would possibly consider meeting me at my crib. I just want to talk to you about the baby and your pregnancy so far, so hit me back when you get a moment, please."

She responded, "I really don't feel like being bothered right now Qamar, this pregnancy has my attitude and hormones on an all time high; I just need some serious time to myself, if you don't mind."

"I do mind Qort, you're carrying my child and you're not allowing me to be a part of the whole experience; not allowing me to even go to appointments with you, nothing. I'm starting to think that you had an abortion and you just don't want to tell me, now I'm only going to tell you one last time that we need to talk, and you need to be at my house within the next fifteen minutes so we can talk like civilized adults, do you hear me?"

"You know what Qamar? I'll come talk to you just so I don't have to hear you bitching and whining anymore, I'm on my way over there now," she replied before abruptly hanging up in my face.

Qortni

Qamar was really starting to irk my nerves and against my better judgment I decided to give in and meet him at his house so he could tell me whatever he needed to talk to me about. I really wasn't feeling the whole idea just on the strength that I'm finally feeling well enough to get some much needed work done that I hadn't been able to get done while I was constantly hugging the toilet.

I decided to meet him at his house 'cause he was actually starting to aggravate the fuck out of me with his constant nagging, bitching, text messages, and oh, calling me was aggravating me more than me throwing up constantly. I got up, showered and headed over to his crib.

"I'm outside," I called and told him when I pulled up.

He came outside, opened my car door and helped me out of the car. I was honest with him and said,

"I really don't feel like going in your house to talk, so we can talk out here," Qamar admitted.

"I got some food cooking on the stove upstairs so we have to go in the crib, it won't take long for me to tell you what I need to talk to you about, I promise."

"Fine Qamar, I don't have the energy to argue with you right now, this baby is kicking my ass in more ways than one."

"You mean the baby you aborted?" he said under his breath but still audible enough for me to hear him.

"Listen, if you're going to start bitching and accusing me of shit I didn't do, I'm leaving."

"Listen Qortni, you not allowing me to be a part of this time in our lives is a bit aggravating, I can't even front. I'm a little pissed that when I wanted to help you when you were on your ass and you pushed me away, it pissed me off. Then I call you the other day to see how you were feeling and to see if you needed anything and you and your cousin have the audacity to be entertaining men, now how fucked up is that? I blocked my number purposely because I knew if I didn't you wouldn't answer my call; and when you do pick up accidentally, there's a man's voice in the background talking to you and your cousin, now start explaining before I lose my temper."

"First of all you need to take all the bass out of your voice, I'm not your child or one of your ex bitches who allowed you to talk to them any ol' way, I'm an adult and you're going to talk to me as one. The male voice you heard in the background the other day was the doctor from the hospital, he was..."

"You fucking bitch!" he yelled at me right before jumping on me and tackling me to the floor of his aunt's kitchen. He had both hands around my neck strangling me; I was slowly but surely losing air. Once he noticed I was going in and out of consciousness he release d his death grip from my neck, and got off me.

I laid on the floor for a good fifteen minutes in pure silence trying to figure out how I went from explaining things to him, to him trying to choke me to death. Once I finally got my breathing under control and I was able to stand without feeling crazy, I didn't utter another word to Qamar, I simply grabbed my keys off of the kitchen table and headed to the front door to leave; I felt him watching my every move but it didn't faze me, I needed to leave because if I didn't he would not only harm me, but he would ultimately harm my child, and I was not around for that, only because I had decided that I was indeed going to keep the baby.

"Where do you think you're going? We haven't finished talking, so I suggest you sit your ass down and not leave until I finish speaking my peace."

"Qamar, I'm not in the right frame of mind right now, you just damn near killed me, and now you want me to sit here and talk to you like we're civilized adults? You have got to be out of your freaking mind. I'm leaving and when I think you're ready to talk and act like a civilized adult, I'll gladly call you so you can finish speaking your peace, now, I'm gone."

"Qort, I'm not playing with you, get ya ass back in here so we can finish talking, I was wrong for putting my hands on you but we need to finish this conversation. You straight up disrespected me by having another man in your bed while you're carrying my child, you don't think that's fucked up?"

"First of all, you didn't just put your hands on me, you fucking tackled me to the damn floor knowing that I'm pregnant, what the fuck is really wrong with you? Like, something is really not clicking in your head right about now, do you know the damage you could have done to my child when you tackled and strangled me? News flash dummy, when you cut off my air supply, you also cut off the air supply to my unborn child, when mommy can't breathe, neither can baby genius!"

I was all the way fed up with his simple acting ass and stupidity; then again I began to wonder if it was all an act or if he was truly missing a hell of a lot of scruples. I was starting to get a headache from all of this going back and forth with him, I was also starting to feel nauseated again and of course I didn't bring my magic pills with me so I really needed to be on my way back to my cousins house to eat, take my pills and lay down.

"Listen Qort, you're not about to be cussing me out in my own crib, and you're right, I was wrong for putting my hands on you in any type of violent manner, now if you just tell me who the man was that you were talking to when you accidentally picked up the phone the other day you can leave and we won't touch this subject again."

"Fine Qamar, the man you heard the other day was the doctor at the hospital that was caring for me, this baby has had me on my ass since I officially found out I was pregnant, the day you were in front of my crib for God only knows what reason. It was the same day Amber went to my house to get me some extra clothes. When she got home she saw me on the floor in her bathroom and that's when she took me to the hospital. Since I hadn't been able to keep any food or liquids down, I went to the hospital to see if I would be able to take something so I can stop losing all this weight and finally be able to eat; happy now?"

"I don't believe you; that man in the background sounded Black and we all know there aren't any Black baby doctors around us in this area, so no, I'm not happy. You could have thought of a better lie to tell."

"Qamar, believe what you want to believe, I'm not about to sit here and argue with you knowing that I'm telling you the truth, you really have some issues that you need help fixing. I'm not around for this shit 'cause it's doing nothing but stressing me the fuck out. I'm leaving and please don't bother calling me anytime soon, we need some time apart, seriously."

I walked out of his aunt's house, and started my way down the stairs from the third floor to the first, when I got halfway down the stairs, right past the second floor apartment Qamar came out of nowhere and pushed me down the remaining stairs.

I tried to break my fall by putting my hands out to at least protect myself, but that didn't work at all, I think I may have broken both of my wrists. To add insult to injury, as if pushing me down fifteen or more stairs wasn't enough, Qamar had the audacity of kneeing me in my stomach countless times while I begged him to stop, not for my sake but for the sake of our baby, but he ignored my pleas and continued to fight me until Nathan and Nature came from God only knows where and got him off of me. Once Nathan was able to get him off me, Nature made certain to keep him a safe distance away from me.

"Qortni, are you okay? What the fuck happened between the two of you?"

"I think I need an ambulance Nate, I feel something wet between my legs and I'm certain I didn't pee on myself, I think I may be bleeding," I told him.

He looked down at my yellow pants and looked back at me, "you are bleeding, I'm calling right now," he told me while pulling out his cell phone.

"911, state your emergency," the operator said through speakerphone.

"Yes, I need an ambulance to 475 Hemmingway Street, I think my cousin's girlfriend is having a miscarriage, she's bleeding heavily."

"I think I may have two broken wrists as well," I added to Nathan's conversation with the ambulance operator.

"There's an ambulance in your area, I'm going to send them right over. Would either of you like to stay on the phone with me until they get there?"

"No, that won't be necessary, I see them coming our way now, thank you," Nathan responded.

As the ambulance pulled up Nature came over and told me he would make sure to keep Qamar away from me, and I asked him to take my phone and call Amberlin for me to let her know I needed her to meet me at the hospital as soon as she could get there. Nathan rode with me and told me he'd stay with me until Amberlin showed up.

"Nathan, thank you for coming when you did, I think had you not shown up when you did, Qamar would have killed me, I appreciate you."

"It's nothing Qortni, trust me, my cousin has had a terrible temper since we were young and dumb. It seems as if it's getting worse and when someone tells him he needs to seek help for it, he dumbs out, so we just don't say shit to him about it. This shit between the both of you a little while ago is unacceptable, especially since you're carrying his seed, I just hope and pray for your sake and the baby's sake that the both of you are alright and that he didn't do too much damage to either one of you."

"Nathan, how did you know I was expecting? It just dawned on me that you told the AMR operator that I might be having a miscarriage.

When did you find out that Qamar and I were expecting? Who else did he tell?" I was firing questions a mile a minute to Nathan. I, now more than ever, prayed that I wasn't having a miscarriage, just on the strength that people in his family may know that he has a child on the way.

"He told me and Nature the same night you told him, I guess you had just left from him when he called us up and told us the news, and knowing my cousin, he's probably told everyone in the family already that there will be a new addition to the family. For someone who just went through all you went through you're sure handling your pain very well, I'd probably be in here crying like a little bitch," Nate responded chuckling.

"If you haven't noticed yet, I'm a tough cookie, it takes a lot for me to break under pressure."

"Dealing with someone like Qamar, you have to be pretty tough; just don't allow your being tough to be the death of you Qort. I know Qamar is my cousin and all but you can do a hell of a lot better than someone like him, don't allow him to break you down."

I allowed his words to sink into my head. Once we pulled up to the hospital, Amber was right in the ambulance bay waiting on me, and I'm not too sure she was supposed to be standing there, but knowing my cousin, she probably cussed out one of the workers at the hospital and they didn't feel like arguing with her so they just let her have her way.

"Qort, I'm about to go back over to Qamar's crib, see what the fuck that dude was thinking, if you need anything call my jack. You still have my number, right Amber?" Nathan asked.

"Yeah, I got it, thanks for looking out for my cousin sweetie, I definitely appreciate it," Amberlin replied.

"Thanks again Nate, I greatly appreciate it, I owe you big time.

"No biggie to either one of you, I'll holla later."

Once I got onto one of the hospital stretchers, one of the techs wheeled me right up to the fourth floor; the maternity floor and one of the maternity nurses check me to make sure the baby was all right.

Dr. Jones came in and also did his own assessment of me and gave me the most pitiful looks I have ever seen on the face of a doctor.

"Ms. Monroe, I'm sorry to have to tell you this but it seems as if you have suffered a miscarriage, can you tell me what happened to you today? Who is responsible for doing this to you?"

I tuned Dr. Jones out after he said I had a miscarriage, I was stunned, hurt, angry, and I wanted revenge on Qamar's ass for taking life from me, the very same life he helped me create. Here I was lying in the hospital having this doctor tell me that my baby was no longer. The baby that I had finally decided to keep was a not too distant memory, my baby was gone.

"Ms. Monroe? Did you hear me?"

"I'm sorry doc, what were you saying?"

"I asked you who was responsible for doing this to you; we have to call the authorities."

I began weeping uncontrollably and Amberlin answered the doctor's question for me.

"The child's father, Qamar Daniels, is the piece of shit that did this to my cousin, and I'm telling you now Travis, the police better to get to him before I do or his family will be making funeral arrangements for his ass."

"I understand your anger Amber but please allow the authorities to handle that bastard, he will get his karma in due time, trust me. Now Qortni, do you have somewhere safe to stay where Mr. Daniels won't be able to bother you? I'm going to put you on bed rest for about a week, and obviously no work for quite some time because of your wrists, which by the way aren't broken, just sprained."

Again Amberlin answered for me, "She'll be staying with me until she feels up to going back to her house. Qamar has no clue as to where I live so she'll be fine."

"Okay, I'm glad to know she has somewhere safe to be. Qortni, please don't have any contact with Mr. Daniels, and please get as much rest as possible. In the next couple of days your bleeding should decrease significantly and within the next two weeks you should be back to normal; and again, I apologize this happened to you. Amberlin, I'll give you a call in a couple of days to see how she's holding up."

"Thank you," were the only two words I was able to utter to Dr. Jones before I started crying again."

Two Days Later

Qamar has been blowing my phone up nonstop with text messages, voicemails, and emails, but I just don't have the energy or patience to deal with him. I fear that if he and I are face to face for any length of time I'm going to try to kill him. I sleep with my ultrasound pictures of my baby every night; kiss it every morning when I wake up and every night before I retire to bed. Both Nathan and Nature keep calling me to check up on me, I'm assuming for Qamar's sake because there are more so his friends than mine. I answer all of their calls for some reason. I guess a part of me feels like I'm indebted to them for saving me so to not answer their calls seems a bit rude to me. Nathan told me that Qamar was taking the news of the miscarriage pretty hard, and that he's never seen Qamar this low in the dumps so to speak. I told him that Qamar couldn't possibly know what I'm feeling because he wasn't the one carrying the baby and he knew exactly what he was doing when he pushed me down the stairs and continually kneed me in my stomach.

"Qort, I know I'm asking a lot of you, but can you at least have a conversation with the man? I understand you're hurting right now, but so is he, he's lost a child too," Nathan asked me.

"Absolutely not, I have nothing to say to him, and if I'm anywhere near him, I'm going to try my hardest to kill him and I'm not trying to be up in Niantic with a bunch of bitches, braiding their hair and all that other nonsense. I'm not in the right frame of mind to deal with him Nathan."

"Fair enough, now I just have one last question, well, Qamar asked me to ask you this so don't bite my head off, he asked me to ask you if you could drop the charges on him. I already told him that you probably wouldn't do it but he asked me to ask you, and I don't want to lie to him and tell him I asked knowing I didn't."

"He's really bugged out and needs to be put in a mental institution, I'm not dropping any charges on him and whatever the outcome of his actions the judge deems sufficient for him, so be it, no one told him to take his anger out on people; he needs help and maybe a little jail time. Let some dudes behind bars show him how it feels to be violated, tell him to go fuck himself," I told Nathan and immediately hit the end button on my phone.

"The fucking nerve of him!" I said to myself.

"What's the matter cuz? Are you all right?" Amberlin asked rushing into the room I was staying in.

"Can you believe that piece of shit, punk ass, sorry excuse of a man had the balls to tell his cousin to ask me if I would be willing to drop the charges on him?"

"Girl, don't pay him any mind, continue to get your rest and don't stress, karma is a bitch and Qamar is definitely going to get what's coming to him. He not only went half on a baby with you, that punk also took the same life that he made with you. I don't see how he sleeps at night; I wouldn't be able to live with myself knowing that I killed an innocent fetus that didn't ask to be conceived; I want to get my hands on him and show him how it feels to be violated," Amberlin told me with tears welling up in her eyes.

"Why are you tearing up? I'm the one that lost the baby."

"Because I have been through this before, not something I wanted you to have to endure, that's why I kept urging you to keep the baby because I know all too well how it feels to lose a child, a fetus with whom you fall in love with the moment you hear their little heart beating and see them on the ultrasound," she responded as she allowed the tears to fall freely down her face.

"Amber, I had no idea, why didn't you tell me? I would have never asked you to come to the hospital with me, I wouldn't have stayed over here to begin with, I'm so sorry, now I really feel like shit," I told her now crying myself, I felt absolutely terrible, and I honestly had no idea.

Just when she was about to respond, her doorbell rang and I was praying Qamar didn't somehow find out where she stayed at because there was definitely going to be a murder scene at her house had he had the audacity to come here.

After going to answer her door, Amberlin came back to the room and told me that she would be out for a few hours and if I needed anything to just call her, I told her I would be fine, she needed to go enjoy herself and not worry about babysitting me tonight. After she left, I got myself into the shower and allowed the warm running water to wash my tears away, I still had a hard time accepting the fact that the baby that was once floating around inside of me is no longer there. I have experienced heartache before, but nothing compared to this. Once I got out of the shower and got comfortable, I put my headphones in my ears and allowed my Jazz playlist to take my thoughts elsewhere until I dozed off.

Qamar

I really fucked up this time, and I don't think Qortni will ever forgive me for this shit and honestly I can't even say that I blame her, I went entirely too far the other day, she won't even take my calls. I called my cousin Nathan to get an update from him on Qort since she wasn't answering any of my phone calls.

"Big cuz, any update on Qortni? Is she feeling any better?"

"What's up man? Yea, I talked to her today, she's still very torn about everything that transpired and she's not dropping the charges on you, in fact, she thinks that a lil bit of jail time is just what you need to see how it feels to be violated. She's really distraught about what happened Q. You fucked up big time this time around and I'm not too sure if you can patch things up between the both of you."

"Fuck. Yo, is there any way you can bring me over to her cousin's house so I can speak to her face to face? I know you're probably getting tired of calling her for me and I need to speak to her since she's not answering any of my phone calls."

"Hell no I'm not bringing you over there, you must really not value your life fam, Qort and Amber are both waiting to get at you for the shit you did, and I'm damn sure not about to be put in a body bag as well by Amber because I brought you to her crib. You're out of your rabid ass mind, she keeps her house location secretive for a reason and I'm not about to violate that, you're better off just waiting until Qort calls you when she's ready to talk to you; which judging by her conversation with me today won't be anytime soon. I personally think you just need to cut your losses and move on with your life, I highly doubt she's going to be coming back to you after this shit right here, I just can't see it to be honest."

"I respect what you're saying Nate but honestly I didn't ask you for your fucking opinion, Qort is my wife to be, she'll be back sooner than later, I just need to give her some time."

"What you need to do is get some help for your fucking anger problems, real shit. I honestly want to whoop ya ass for that mess, how do you sleep at night knowing that you caused the woman who you supposedly love, care about and want to marry so much hurt? How do you sleep at night knowing that the child you helped create is the same child you killed two days ago because of your insecurity? Do me a favor Q, don't call my phone anymore until you get some help for your problems, I don't even want to be associated with you right now until you seek help," Nathan told me before hanging up right in my ear.

I called Nature's phone to see what he was up to and to see if he would be able to call Qort for me to see if she would be willing to meet me in public somewhere tomorrow so we could talk. I miss seeing her, I miss being around her and I miss not being able to be there for her, supporting her through this tough time, even if I am to blame for her anguish and misery right now.

"Q, what's good my boy? What's going on?"

"Nothing much man, just got into an argument with Nate about the shit gong on now between Qortni and myself. I called you to see if you would be willing to do me a favor?"

"I'm down to help you out, as long as I don't have to get in the middle of what's going on between you and Qortni, I'm not trying to get mixed up in the middle of that shit, you hurt her real bad man."

"I hear what you're saying man but I just need one small favor, I just need for you to call and ask her if she'd be willing to meet me in public somewhere tomorrow morning so her and I can talk and try to work through all of this shit."

I'll call but this is the one and only time I'm going to call her for you, I'm not around for her cussing me out for doing your dirty work, text me her number and after I call her I'll call you back and tell you what she said."

I gave Nature Qortni's number and impatiently waited for him to call me back to tell me what she said, even though I already knew she was going to say absolutely not, but shit, it was worth a try; Nature called me back about five minutes later.

"So, what did she say? Was she cool with meeting me somewhere in person?"

"Damn, calm your thirsty ass down, she didn't answer the phone, it just rang and rang, but no answer so l left her a message, told her to hit my jack when she got the message, so hopefully she'll call me back before the evening is over with and if she does, I'll hit you back, aight?"

"Aight man, hit me back as soon as you hear from her, I'm going to see if her parents have heard from her or can help me out."

"I thought her family didn't care for you. You really think they're going to help you get in contact with her or help you get her back after the shit you put her through?"

"No, they don't care for me but I'm desperate right now and I'm willing to at least try to get some information from them, I'll hit you back later."

After hanging up with Nature, I decided against calling Qortni's parents so I borrowed my aunt's car and went over to Qortni's parent's house to see if they could help me get in contact with Qort and to see if they could talk her into dropping these charges against me.

"Good afternoon Mr. Monroe, is it possible for me to speak to you and Mrs. Monroe for a moment?"

"Hello Qamar, the Mrs. isn't home and neither is Qortni. Is there anything I can help you with?"

"I was wondering if you could help me out with something. Qortni and I got into an argument a couple of days ago and the end result wasn't so pretty if you know what I mean."

He crossed his hands across his chest, raised is eyebrow and said, "No, I don't know what you mean, care to explain?"

"Well, I allowed my anger to get the best of me and when she was leaving my house I pushed her down some stairs and she ended up miscarrying the child we were expecting, and I'm coming to you to ask if you would be able to help me get back in good standing with her, I messed up terribly and she won't accept any of my calls. I wanted to know if you would be able to talk to her for me to see if she would possibly consider at least having a face to face conversation with me, I'm desperate sir."

"Wait, let me get this straight, you and my daughter have an argument, you get mad when she tries to leave and your punk ass puts your hands on her and she ends up having a miscarriage? Being that you know you messed up you come over to my house to see if my wife and I can help you get back in good standing with her because she's not answering any of your phone calls? You are responsible for killing my unborn grandchild and you want my help? Qamar, let me tell you something, I'm not too fond of you, never have been and most likely never will be, to answer your question; and hell no I won't help you get in contact with my daughter. You have balls just for coming over here and having the nerve to ask me such a question. I suggest you step up off my porch right now before I allow my anger to get the best of me and I whoop your ass," he told me then closed the door right in my face.

I have exhausted all of my resources. Nathan won't help me anymore because he said he doesn't blame Qortni for not wanting to speak to me or drop the charges against me. Nature sounds like he's about to be siding with Nathan and I kind of already knew Qort's parents weren't going to be of any assistance just on the strength that neither one of them care for me. I guess I'm just going to have to wait it out until she feels like contacting me again. I can't even call the female that I once considered my best friend because I cut her loose after she got me fucked up in the club.

Since I was bored with nothing to do I decided to call my father up and chill with him for a little while since I haven't spent too much time with him lately, I also wanted to pick his brain on how to make things right between me and Qortni, since he has known Qortni since she was born.

Amberlin

I didn't expect to start crying in front of Qortni, shit I didn't even expect to tell her that I had suffered a miscarriage. That was something I thought I would take to the grave with me; but seeing the pain she was in even before she had the miscarriage brought me back to the time I was going through mine. Unlike Qortni, I didn't have anyone to help me through my grieving process, which I only have myself to blame for it because I didn't tell anyone, except for my boyfriend at the time, which happened to be Nathan. I don't even think Qortni even knows that Nathan and I used to date one another, something else I kept from her, I'm sure I'll tell her one day though.

Anyhow, seeing Nathan over the past few months since Qortni and Qamar have been dealing with one another, old sparks between him and I started to arise and we have been trying to see if we can rekindle an old flame.

"So, I hear Qamar wants my cousin to drop the charges against him, is he serious?"

"Serious as a heart attack, but I told her in the ambulance the other day that she can do better and she needs to not allow Qamar to be her downfall; Qamar has a serious anger problem and he needs some serious help, he's had this problem since we were young and it's getting worse by the day. He got mad at me today because I told him I wasn't going to be the mediator between the two of them anymore because I don't blame Qort for the way she's feeling, and he blew up at me, but oh well, it is what it is."

"Yeah, she was spazzing after you and her got off the phone when you came to pick me up, I told her karma is going to get Qamar better than any of us can, but I can't front, I want to whoop his ass so bad right now, I still can't believe my cousin lost the baby," I replied to Nathan getting teary eyed again.

"C'mon shorty, don't cry, you about to have me up in here crying with you, you know I think about our seed everyday, and I think that's why I was in such a hurry to help Qortni out when she and Qamar got into it, I knew that feeling all too well. Anyhow, on a brighter note being that we've eaten, what do you want to do now?"

"Let's go back to my crib, I need to check on Qort, she hasn't called but she's so stubborn that if she did need something she wouldn't call anyhow. If she's doing alright we can go to the movies or something."

"That's cool with me," he responded while taking his phone out.

"No talking to your sidepieces, it's my time now," I told him half joking.

"Nah, Nature just hit me up talking about Qamar, I guess he went to your aunt and uncle's house to see if either one of them could help him get back right with her and ya uncle spazzed on him." I broke out laughing, laughing so hard I had tears coming out of my eyes. That fool had officially lost his damn mind; did he really think my family was going to help him get back with her? No one and I do mean no one in my family likes his ass, dummy.

"I'm surprised my uncle didn't whoop his ass, my uncle is quick tempered as well, especially when it comes to any of his kids."

"I'm not getting in the middle of that shit and if Nature is smart he would tell Qamar he's not getting in the middle of anything as well, Qamar needs to just allow Qortni to heal and if by any chance she gives him a second chance, he better cherish it."

"I honestly think Qortni is going to give him another chance, maybe not right away but soon, I know my cousin and she's glutton for punishment, but it's her life, I'm not going to judge her. I just hope and pray if they do get back together they don't experience another miscarriage; that won't be cool because I may actually have to whoop Qamar's ass for real if he puts her through that again."

"Definitely feel you on that shorty."

After Nathan and I ate, we went back to my house to check up on Qortni and she was sound asleep, but her phone kept ringing so I took it upon myself to answer it. What the hell did I do that for? It was my uncle and to say he was pissed was an understatement, he was hurt to hear that his baby girl had a miscarriage and had to find out through the father and killer of the baby. He was even more pissed because his daughter didn't think she could come to him and her mother and tell them what was going on. So, I told him that was something that the three of them would have to get together and talk about, that was not my battle to fight.

Neither Nathan nor I really felt like going to the movies after we got back to my house so we decided to just chill in my room and watch movies, and of course we both dozed off.

A year and a half later...
Qortni

A year has passed by since Qamar and I had the fight and lost our baby. I stopped all communication with him for about a month and a half just so I could get my mind right and become one with myself. I took Nathan's words to heart and thought long and hard about the relationship Qamar and I were in and where it was headed.

After ignoring countless messages and phone calls from Qamar, I finally gave into his pleas and met him somewhere in public during the day so he and I could talk, and as crazy as it may seem, after he and I talked for about three hours, with me crying, punching, kicking and yelling at him, we both mutually decided to give our relationship another try. So far, it's been pretty good, we've had minor arguments, only one time got a little physical and that was the night of the Super Bowl, he was a little drunk and he got mad at a comment I made and started pulling my hair; but other than that we're in a good place. Even though we're still pretty young, the topic of marriage has come up, he says he wants to marry me, but I told him he must get some help for his temper first. I refuse to marry anyone who has a temper as bad as his. Many of you may be asking, well why is this chick in a relationship with someone who has caused her so much hurt and pain, then she has the nerve to be considering marrying him as long as he gets help? Well, to answer your question, I'm still in deep like with Qamar, he loves me, so why not give him another shot?

Ever since Qamar and I have been back together he's become quite the romancer, doing spontaneous things for me just because and I'm enjoying all of it, although I'm not too sure where he's getting the money to do all of this since he's still unemployed. Hey, I'm not going to say anything about it because it's not coming out of my pockets so I'm just going to keep enjoying all that he does for me. Valentine's Day is a week away and Qamar told me to make sure I leave work on time so I can meet up with him later that evening for a special night; I'm a little apprehensive because since the day he caused me to miscarry I haven't spent an overnight with him anywhere; my nerves haven't allowed me to be that comfortable with him yet, but I'm thinking I need to get over it. I know he's going to want me to stay the night with him on Valentine's Day and it would be very rude of me not to.

Valentine's Evening

"**H**ey shorty, just checking in on you to make sure you're going to be able to leave work on time so we can meet up tonight, I have a very special surprise for you that I know you're going to just love," Qamar texted me.

I responded, "Hey sweetie, I'm leaving work now and I'm on my way home to shower and get dressed. What kind of attire should I dress in?"

"Great to hear. Dress in something sexy, not too dressy, but not too casual, something like semi-formal, cute dress, heels, you know how you do. I'll pick you up at your house in about two hours. I'll call you when I'm on my way."

"Okay, I'll be ready and waiting."

After I finished texting Qamar, I called Amberlin to see if she could help me do my hair before Qamar came over to get me.

"Hey hoe, what's going on with ya? I need a small favor."

"What's going on trick? I just got in from the mall, what ya need?"

"I need for you to help me do my hair, Qamar said he'll be over here in two hours to pick me up, I just need something simple and quick."

"I just passed by your house, I'll bust a U-turn and I'll be there in like two minutes, meet me at the front door, I can try my new clothes on in your room."

"Aight, I'm coming down now."

Once Amber got to the house I took my shower while she was trying on her new clothes. She and Nathan had a date tonight as well. As you can imagine, I was quite surprised when I learned about Nathan and Amberlin being a couple, but I wasn't mad. They make a cute couple, they compliment each other very well.

"So, what are you and Nate getting into tonight?" I asked her while she was in the bathroom with me trying on one of her five new outfits.

"I don't know what he has planned, I honestly don't know how he'll be able to top what he's been doing for the past year since we linked back up; but whatever it is he has planned, I'm sure I'm going to love it, he's so damn romantic."

"I feel you on that mama; I'm a little nervous about spending the night with Qamar tonight, this will be the first time since I had the miscarriage that I'm going to spend the night with him. I'm scared shitless, my heart still doesn't trust him completely."

"If you don't trust him, then why are you with him?"

I waited until I got out of the shower to answer her question, "I'm in very deep like with him, he loves me though, and he says he wants to marry me. I still think there's hope for us. Hopefully I can one day love him like he loves me, it's just that the day I suffered the miscarriage still haunts me like it was just yesterday."

"Girl, you about to have me crying up in here, but I completely understand what you're saying; you have to ask yourself is this what you want? Do you want to continue on in a relationship with him knowing that it's going to take you a while to get over what happen to you a year ago? Your wounds haven't completely healed."

"I hear you cuz, and I appreciate your words," I told her while drying off and putting my robe on. "I'm praying I don't have a serious meltdown tonight while he and I are out, that would kill the whole mood. He would hate me after that!" I laughed.

"You're nuts, you have serious issues, he would definitely hate you for that, especially since he's been trying to get back on your good side for the longest. How are your parents feeling about the both of you being back together?"

"Neither one of them are happy about it, but they kind of know better than to say too much to me about it; you know the three of us don't get along so their opinions don't really matter to me. They both were more so pissed that I didn't tell them I was pregnant and that I'm out here having sex. They were hurt that they had to find out about my pregnancy from Qamar but shit, it is what is it, and you know none of your cousins aren't overly fond of him either."

"Understandably, I still can't stand the bastard my damn self but I tolerate him on the strength of you and because he's Nathan's cousin, even though Nathan really doesn't deal with him like that anymore since that day. So, how are we styling your hair? Up-do, loose curls, tight curls?"

"Let's do some Shirley Temple curls, not too lose though, I need my hair to last me for a while."

"Cool, it's not going to take me long to do them, and you think you're slick. I don't know why you said you wanted me to help you do your hair, you know damn well you weren't going to help me, you want me to do it all for you, but it's cool, 'cause when I finish your hair you're going to do mine for me; fair enough exchange right?"

"That's cool with me, 'cause I already have my outfit out and ready."

After Amberlin did my hair and I did hers, we both got dressed, and since Nathan had told Amber he'd be here to pick her up around the same time Qamar was picking me up, she told him to pick her up from my house; I mean it only made sense.

At Dinner

"**Y**ou look absolutely stunning babe, you definitely outdid yourself tonight," Qamar told me as we were being seated in Ruth's Chris Steakhouse.

"Thank you, I have Amber to thank for my hair, my outfit is compliments of me," I told him smiling; I was trying to hide my nervousness.

"Next time you talk to Amber tell her I said kudos to her for her skills with doing hair. Qort, I really want to thank you for agreeing that I could take you out tonight and show you how much I care about you and love you. I know it probably was a hard decision for you to make, but I'm glad you decided yes. I have a whole lot planned for you tonight; I want to show you that I'm serious about us and that I have changed in the past year, for the better of course.

"Honestly Qamar, I'm nervous as hell about tonight, this will be the first time since we got back together that I'll be spending the night with you, and I'm not too comfortable with the idea. I've been treading on very thin ice with you for the past year; if I disagree with something you do or say for fear that you're going to hit me or worse, try to kill me. The scar on my heart from the loss of my baby is still fresh as the day it happened."

"I totally understand Qortni, that's why I have taken the initiative and signed up for some anger management classes to help me focus in on what is making me so angry so I can release it all and become a better person, a better boyfriend to you and in the long run better husband material."

"That's nice to hear Q, but let's not talk marriage too soon, I mean we're still young, we still have our whole lives ahead of us, no need to rush marriage, let's just take things one day at a time."

After ordering dinner and eating we got in the car and headed to Qamar's next surprise for me.

"Thanks for dinner babe, it was beautiful and thank you for my bouquet of flowers, they are absolutely stunning, where are we headed to now?"

"Only the best for my future wife, and our next destination is a surprise, if I tell you it'll ruin the whole surprise."

"Can I ask you a question?"

"Shoot."

"Um, where did you get the money to do all of this? I mean Ruth's Chris isn't a cheap restaurant and I'm pretty sure the rest of the evening's surprise is pretty costly."

"Don't worry your pretty little head about where I got the money for this; tonight, just bask in all that I have planned for you."

To avoid an argument, I simply replied, "As you wish."

When he told me we were about fifteen minutes away from the next destination he pulled out a blindfold from his coat pocket and asked me to put it on, I wasn't comfortable at all with his request and I think my facial expression told him so.

"Babe, please, I don't want to ruin the surprise for you, as soon as we get to where we're going you can take it off, I promise it's nothing to be scared of, please trust me on this?"

"Fine, give me the blindfold."

He handed me the blindfold and I put it on carefully making sure not to mess up my hair.

"Alright babe, we're here, now stay still so I can help you out of the car and to the front of where we're going."

"Ok, just don't make me fall; these heels and dress are very expensive."

He helped me out the car and to the front of wherever we were at and I was beginning to shiver a little 'cause I was standing outside of God knows where in a tube top styled dress, obviously a dumb move on my part. Once he opened what sounded like a door, he helped me over the threshold and took my blindfold off of me.

"Surprise baby, all of this is for you tonight, champagne, chocolate covered strawberries, the big teddy bear, and the Jacuzzi over in the corner, Happy Valentine's Day baby. I love you."

To say I was disgusted was an understatement, he had all the right things inside of the hotel room but the hotel, or motel rather was a complete turnoff, it seems as if he found the cheapest motel he could find, the floors had a nasty looking rug that looked to be over a hundred years old, there was a ridiculous stench coming from the bathroom, the Jacuzzi looked like it hadn't been clean since the first day it was installed.

"Baby, can I be honest with you for a moment without you getting overly upset?"

"Sure, it's your day, what's up?"

"This room we're in is a hot ass mess, I don't even think this place could be classified as a motel, do you mind taking me home?"

"Are you fucking serious? I went out of my way to have a few of my people set this room up for you and you're now asking me to take you home? You need to find your own way home because I'm not taking your ungrateful ass anywhere. I try to do something special for you and this is the thanks I get? Bitch please, miss me with that bullshit."

I blinked my eyes trying to figure out if I was seeing things, adjusted my ears to figure out if I were hearing things, did he just call me a bitch? I didn't even have the energy to argue with him; instead I went outside, opened my cell phone and called a friend of mine to see if he was able to pick me up.

"Hey Jay, it's Qortni, I hope I'm not interrupting you or anything."

"Hey Qortni, nah you're not interrupting me, what's going on? Is everything all right? I thought you were going out with ya man tonight?"

"I did, I am, well I did go out with him and we just got into an argument and he's not trying to take me home and I was wondering if it's possible for you to meet me at the Athenian Diner over on Whalley Ave?"

"Yeah, no problem, I'll be there in about five minutes, stand inside the restaurant, it's late and it's cold outside."

"Ok, I'll be in there waiting on you, thank you so much Jaison, I definitely appreciate. I'll be in the front of the diner waiting on you."

As I started walking toward the diner, Qamar came outside to see where I was and to tried to apologize for calling me out of my name, but the damage was already done.

"Qortni, where are you going? It's too late to be out here walking, I'll take you home."

"I'm fine, I have someone coming to pick me up, don't worry about me, I hope you enjoy the rest of your night, better yet, I hope you enjoy the rest of your life, I'm done Qamar, I can't do this anymore, enough is enough."

"Qortni, please don't do this to me, to us, I said I was sorry, can you please stop walking so we can talk?"

"No Qamar, now please leave me alone! I don't want to be bothered with you any longer, your temper is ridiculous and you just called me out of my fucking name! I can't anymore, I just can't. I don't have the energy to do it and there's no sense in us trying to force something to work knowing damn well it's not working; so we might as well just cut our losses now and move on with our lives separately."

"I love you Qortni, I really do," he told me, but I turned a deaf ear to his cries and pleas, I was tired of going through this shit with him so instead of getting into a physical fight with him, I just thought it best for me to leave, I could handle getting into a verbal altercation with him, but I couldn't stomach getting into anything physical with him.

As I finally made it to the front of the diner, Jaison was just pulling up, so I walked over to his car and he opened the door for me, talk about perfect timing.

"Jaison, thank you so much for coming to pick me up, I really hope I didn't interrupt you or your evening."

"You're good ma, you didn't interrupt anything. I was watching television when you called me, stop worrying, are you going to your house?"

"Yeah, I just need to get some clothes and pick my car up, I'm going to have to stay at my cousin's house tonight, I don't want my crazy ass ex to show up at my house tonight or tomorrow."

"Ex? You and ol boy broke up? What the hell happened tonight if you don't mind me asking?"

"Everything was fine in the beginning, dinner was great, he gave me flowers and everything, then he thinks he's surprising me by bringing me to the damn Regal Inn to end the night, the room was extra low budget, I couldn't stay in that room another second. Then he got mad at me because I asked him if he minded taking me home; he called me a bitch and that's when I left to call you. I didn't have the energy to get into a physical altercation with him tonight, I have had enough of his shit, and the fact that I still don't fully trust him doesn't help either."

"Damn Ma, sorry to hear that. Would you like to stay at my crib tonight? I have a guest bedroom that doesn't get used."

"You sure you don't mind? I don't really want to impose on you, and I really don't want to stay at my cousin's house, she and her man are probably going back over there tonight to end their evening."

"If I minded I wouldn't have offered. I'll bring you by your crib so you can get whatever clothes you need and then we can go to my crib, you can even follow me there with your car if that makes you feel any better."

"Are you absolutely certain I won't be imposing on you? I don't want to be a bother."

"Qort, listen to me, if you were going to be imposing or a bother I wouldn't have offered it to you in the first place. Now, I'm taking you home so you can get whatever you need to stay at my crib and so you can get your car."

"Thank you so much Jaison, you don't know how much of a life saver you are to me right now, I definitely appreciate you for this!"

Jaison brought me home to grab my overnight bag and my car and I followed him to his house, seems like he and Amberlin had the same thing in mind when looking for a house, they both wanted to be somewhere not too many people would be able to find them. I know I wouldn't be able to find his house again if I had to do it by myself. Anyhow, once I got to his house I took a shower and got comfortable and it wasn't until I saw Jaison in clothes outside of his work uniform did I realize how fine he was. I mean I always had a thing for him secretly but damn, this dude is built like a damn Adonis. He was in his living room watching a movie on his couch and I asked if he wanted some company.

"Would you like some company?"

"Sure, why not? I'm watching *Ray*, with Jamie Foxx."

"Oh God, I love that movie! Jamie Foxx did the damn thing; he must have studied Ray Charles for a while to get into character."

"Hell yeah, he rocked Ray Charles' character, if Ray could see it I think he'd definitely be pleased."

"Definitely."

"Are you hungry? I'm about to go pop some popcorn, do you want anything?"

"Do you have wine? I'm in the mood for some wine right about now, after this shitty ass day I need something to wind me down."

"I sure do, I keep my bar downstairs stocked, you can go help yourself or you can bring a bottle or two up if you like."

"Cool."

Once he popped the popcorn and I brought the wine up, we continued watching Ray and before we knew it we had gone through both bottles; we both fell asleep on his living room couch.

One Week later

It's been a week since Qamar and I broke up and surprisingly he hasn't tried to contact me, thank God. I really feel good about him and I breaking up, I'm less stressed and I don't have a care in the world. Jaison has been the perfect host while I stayed at his house, but I told him this morning that I will be going back to my house tonight because I don't want to wear out my welcome; I can't hide from Qamar forever, I have a life to live and so does Jaison.

I hadn't talked to Amberlin since Valentine's Day, and she doesn't even know about the bullshit I went through with Qamar, so I decided to call her to see if she wanted to meet me somewhere for breakfast and fill her in on the events that led up to Qamar and I breaking up again. She agreed to meet me so we could catch up.

"Hey girl how was your night with Qamar? Did he go all out for you?"

"Girl, him and I broke up on that night, he treated me to a great dinner at Ruth's Chris steakhouse, then this nut brings me to the damn Regal Inn with a dirty stench smelling room that was decorated. The Jacuzzi was dirty as hell, looking like it hadn't been cleaned since the day it was installed. The bathroom was a freaking mess, I just couldn't; and when I asked him kindly to take me home, he called me ungrateful, told me to find my own way home and to top it all off, he called me a bitch."

She began laughing hysterically, and I couldn't be mad at her, I began laughing as well. She told me once she partially composed herself, "Wait, not the dingy ass Regal Inn? That dude is ridiculous and not for nothing but y'all could have had dinner at Chili's or something and the money he would have saved by not going to Ruth's Chris he could have gotten you a real room at a real hotel, sometimes I wonder if he and Nathan are really related 'cause they act so different from one another."

96

"Ain't that the truth? He and I broke up the same night, I called a friend of mine from work to come pick me up and thankfully Qamar hasn't tried to call or contact me since that night."

"He's really bugged out, has he been to any anger management classes? He definitely needs them."

"Hell no, he said he would start taking them but he's done nothing yet, and quite frankly I don't care anymore. I'm done and I'm washing my hands of him and all of the bullshit that comes along with him, I can't do it any more, I'm tired."

"I feel you mama, I'm sorry you had to go through that, how come you didn't call me or Nathan? We would have come to get you."

"I didn't want to impose on y'all; my friend that I called said he wasn't busy so he was able to come get me. I feel as if I've been a bother to you enough already with my drama a year ago so I was trying to use other resources, but trust if my friend wasn't able to pick me up, I would have called you and Nathan."

"Listen to me Qort, you are never a bother to me and you're never imposing on me, you're family and family comes first so trust me when I tell you, if you ever need me, no matter the time or place I'm always around for you."

"Thank you mama, I definitely appreciate it, now, how was your Valentine's evening? I know Nathan went all out for you, it's been what, a year since y'all have been together?"

"Yes, it's been a year and some change and yes, he did go all out for me, and guess what!"

Before I could even ask her what he did, she took her left hand out of her pocket and planted right on her left ring finger was a gorgeous princess cut white gold diamond that was damn near blinding me, I was so happy for her!

"Congrats girl, oh my God, I'm so happy for you! You know I'm going to be your maid of honor, have ya'll set a date yet?"

"Thank you cuz, he totally caught me off guard with the proposal, like I wasn't even expecting it. We ended up spending the evening in New York, we ate at the Four Seasons restaurant, had a horse and carriage ride through Central Park, it was just amazing. He proposed during our horse and carriage ride and he did it in a very big way. Girl, who would have thought that your misfortune would bring Nathan and I back together, not saying that I'm happy you went through what you went through but had it not been for that I wouldn't have started talking to Nathan again and I would have been missing out on what a great guy he's turned out to be. In a weird, twisted way I have you to thank for bringing him and I together, so thank you cuz."

I began tearing up, just the thoughts of what happened that terrible day a year and some change ago, my baby would be here, I would be a little happier with my life, except for the fact that I would still have to deal with Qamar. I told Amberlin I would talk to her a little later, so I paid for my tab and left the restaurant. I decided to call Jaison so he could direct me back to his house; Lord knows I couldn't get there by myself. Once I got to his house I packed my overnight bag and told Jaison that I was very grateful for him allowing me to stay with him for the past couple of days.

"You know you don't have to leave now right? I have been enjoying your company for the past couple of days, I'm going to be lonely without you," Jay told me with the most pitiful looking face and sad puppy dog eyes.

"I don't want to overstay my welcome, I have enjoyed your company as well and I truly appreciate everything you did for me two days ago, but I need to stop hiding from Qamar and get on with my life."

"How about you spend one more night over here, we can go bowling, skating or to the movies or just chill to talk, just one more night please?"

I couldn't resist is invitation, so of course I accepted.

"Okay, why not, one more night isn't going to kill me. We should go bowling, I haven't been bowling in a while and plus I don't skate."

"Bowling it is then, I hope you brought your A game 'cause I'm kind of nice in bowling, and even though it's been a minute, I'm sure I still have my skills," he told me smiling.

"We shall see tonight then; I'm about to go take a quick shower and change into something more comfortable, I'll be ready in about fifteen minutes."

"That's cool Ma, I'm about to hop in the shower myself."

Once Jaison and I finally decided to call it quits at bowling, we had bowled at least ten games and he was the victorious one, beat me by two games. I had a lot of fun with him tonight, and neither one of us wanted the night to end.

"Care to join me for dinner tonight?"

"You know me too well to know I never turn down an invitation for food. Where are we dining tonight?"

"I'm thinking *Friday's*. I love their teriyaki chicken pasta and their drinks are on point, you game?"

"Hell yeah I'm game, and dinner is my treat tonight," I responded while we were walking to the car.

"Nah shorty, I can't ask you to pay for dinner, that's not a good look on my end."

"You didn't ask me to pay, I offered and I'm not taking no for an answer, I'm paying and that's that."

He looked at me sideways, smiled and said, " I like your style Qortni, and I've been seeing a side of you that I don't get to see at work, you're cooler than I initially thought. Any man that lets you go is a dummy, real talk. You're the type of female that holds a man down no matter what, I dig that, and whatever man is blessed enough to marry you in the future is definitely going to be a lucky man."

"Aw, Jay, you're making me blush. I like to think I'm a unique type of girl, and I think one of the biggest problems I face when dealing with guys is the fact that they see how hard I hustle out here for my bread and they see it as a threat of some sort and they shouldn't. The way I see it, if we're in a relationship together, then we hold each other down, but a lot of guys don't see it like that."

"The guys who don't see it like that aren't real men, they're boys who don't deserve to be called a real man, and not for nothing Qort. Please don't take what I'm about to say the wrong way, but I always thought you were too good for Qamar, he's a herb, the dude has nothing going for himself, he's basically a bum and you could do so much better than him."

"It's crazy 'cause you sound just like my cousin Amber and his cousin Nathan telling me that shit, I know it's not a coincidence it's something I need to take heed to and that's another reason I ended it with him, he has too many insecurities and he's too damn over protective. I'm not around for that, and not to sound conceited but I know I'm not an ugly chick, I can basically get any guy I want. I don't know what it is about Qamar that kind of draws me to him, I think when I have to deal with him I'm high all the time, real rap."

"Well, they're right ma, and once you find a man on your level who not only supports your endeavors and who grinds as hard as you, but who also uplifts you and pushes you to be more and helps you reach your goals, you're going to be unstoppable."

"I can't believe you're making me blush, can we start drinking now? I need some alcohol in my system, you're sitting here making me too emotional, we're supposed to be enjoying ourselves tonight and not talking about my past. Let's go have a seat over there at the bar and let's start drinking, and before you even ask, no I'm not old enough legally to drink but I know a couple of the bartenders here so I'm good money," I told him laughing as we walked into the restaurant.

Jaison and I stayed at the restaurant and ate and drank for at least three hours and it's a good thing his house is literally ten minutes away from the restaurant or else we would have been hit. Once we made it back to his house we both crashed on his living room couch. He turned the television on and I picked a random movie for us to watch and before I knew what was going on Jaison and I were tonguing each other down. I straddled his lap and was helping him remove his shirt, and he gladly returned the favor and helped me out of my clothes. The alcohol we consumed not too long ago was definitely having an effect on us and I wasn't mad at that at all. I was enjoying every moment of having Jaison's hands all over me, his mouth all over me, shit, I just felt good in general, not a care in the world.

"Qortni, I want you so bad right now, but if you're not comfortable doing this, I understand and I'll stop, just say the word," he told me in between kisses.

"Jaison, I want you and you want me so just stop talking and take me, I'm all yours tonight baby," I responded to him in between planting soft kisses from his head down his chest. Before I could say anything else Jaison had flipped me over on to the couch from his lap, had my legs spread eagle and placed his head in between my legs and began to feast on my pussy like it was his last meal. He was definitely talented at eating me out and I was enjoying every second of it. On one hand I didn't want him to stop but on the other hand if he was this thorough at eating me out then God only knows how talented he is with his dick.

"Damn Jay, you're eating this pussy right, I haven't had head this good in a long time."

"You like that? How well do you like it baby?"

"I like it a lot baby, but I want to feel your dick inside of me right now; you got my pussy extra wet."

"You sure you ready for this dick baby? I don't think you're ready for it."

"Give it to me now babe! Stop teasing me and just put it..."

Before I could even finish my sentence, he rammed his dick into me and I'll be damned if he wasn't right, I don't think I was ready for it, he was so damn big, bigger than Qamar by a long shot.

Jaison and I must have had sex for a whole hour and I lost count as to how many times he made me cum; up until now I thought something was wrong with me because I never came when Qamar and I had sex, so Jaison confirmed for me that indeed nothing was wrong with me; after we fucked we fell asleep in each other's arms right on his living room couch.

Qamar

I fucked up royally with Qortni and I don't think there is any way I can come back from how I dumbed out on her and called her a bitch on Valentine's evening but she really pissed me off when she insulted the room I had my people's decorate for her and then she had the audacity to ask me to bring her home; doesn't she realize she is the only female I have even done some shit like this for? I mean what normal female would act like that when their man has gone out of his way to make her evening as special as I did for her? I haven't tried contacting her because I know she's going to have a mouthful of choice words for me and I'm not really sure I'm ready for them, so I'm just allowing her some time to cool down so I can talk to her like a civilized adult.

I'm still trying to figure out who she got to pick her up that night, I know it wasn't Amberlin nor Nathan, unless one of them got a new ride; I started to follow whoever it was but I thought better of it, I don't know the person and if by chance it was another man I'm not sure if dude was carrying or not, and I wasn't chancing that. The way she left and didn't even want to hear what I had to say, a little voice in my head was telling me that I lost her for good. I need someone else's opinion on the whole situation, someone who is from the outside looking in to shed some light on the situation, but I have no clue as to who that would be, I need to do something to let Qortni know she's my world and to get her back, one thing for sure, and two's for certain, I will not rest until she is mine, 'cause the way I look at it, if I can't have her no one else can, and I'll die making sure she's mine for good.

Amberlin

I don't know if it was something I did or said to Qortni that made her just up and leave me at the restaurant the other day, but the way she left just didn't sit right with me. I haven't talked to her since that day, and that's not like us not to communicate at least once a day, let alone go a few days without speaking. I hope she didn't take my comment about her small misfortune being my blessing to the heart, I honestly didn't mean to come out the face like that, but shit, it's true; had Qamar not done what he did to her, Nathan and I probably wouldn't have rekindled the love we once thought was long gone. Now don't get me wrong, I am by no means happy about the fact that Qortni lost her child but I am happy that Nathan and Nature were there to help her, shit, she should be happy for me, I've finally found real love. Since I haven't heard from her, I decided to be the bigger person and call her so she could meet me at my crib and we could talk about whatever is bothering either one of us face to face over a glass or two of wine.

"Qort, it's Amber, if you're not busy, can you come over to my house for about an hour or so?"

"Yeah, I can do that, you ready for me to come over now?"

"Yes, now is cool, I won't hold you up too long."

"Okay, I'll be over shortly; I'm not too far from your house."

"Just use your key to get in; I'll be waiting for you."

Once I got off the phone with her, I ran around the corner to the liquor store to grab a couple of bottles of wine since Nathan and I had gone through all the alcohol in my house when we celebrated our engagement. When I got back to the house Qortni was just then pulling up, so we walked in together.

"Hey girl, how are you?" Qortni asked me once we got into the house.

"I'm good girl, how are you?"

"I'm good, better yet, I'm great!"

"Well damn, I haven't seen you this happy in a long time, what or shall I ask who has you all happy and glowing?"

"Jaison is responsible for me being happy and glowing, he's such a gentleman."

"I'm glad you're happy Qort, but please don't go rushing into anything with him. You and Qamar just broke up good and you're already jumping in bed with another guy, slow down Qort, are you completely sure you're over Qamar?"

"Yes I'm completely sure, I can't be with him anymore, I'm tired of being his human punching bag, his garbage disposal in which he would empty his kids into while we were fucking, I'm tired of him imagining I'm one of his side hoes and him calling their name out while I'm sexing him. I'm just tired of him period and there's no coming back for him with me. Our relationship ended the day he pushed me down the stairs and I lost my baby, I can't do it anymore. He straight disrespected me in ways no female should be disrespected. I can only take but so much of his shit and besides, I don't love him, he was a cool person when we met, but I don't love him neither am I in love with him, I'm merely with him to boost his confidence up, it's the least I could do for him."

"I just don't want you to end up hurt or end up hurting Jaison in the end, it just seems as if he's your rebound guy, the perfect man in the most fucked up time, but those are just my thoughts, now on to why I asked you to come over today. A couple of days ago we were at the restaurant, in which you invited me to so we could talk, and after I had some words with you, you threw the money on the table to pay for your tab then you walked out on me like the conversation we were having was done; what the hell was up with that cause I'm feeling like I missed the memo on something?"

"You're right, I did leave you rather abruptly and it wasn't right but some of the things you were saying that day at the restaurant had me very vexed, like why the hell would you come out of you mouth with some shit about my miscarriage brought you and Nathan together again? Do you not realize that me having a miscarriage a year and a half ago still hurts me to the core? It seems as if you are celebrating the fact that I lost my baby instead of sympathizing with me, it's like I don't know who you are anymore."

"Qort, I apologize if my words hurt you but I was merely telling you what I felt, sorry for being fucking honest! I didn't realize how badly losing your baby hurt you. I mean shit, you didn't even want to keep the baby in the first place, then when you lost it your whole demeanor and attitude changed, what the hell was up with that?"

"Are you freaking kidding me? Are you hearing the bogus shit coming out of your mouth right now? I lost a child, no matter if I decided to abort it or if I had a miscarriage, I lost the child that was growing inside of me and if I'm not mistaken, any human with feelings would feel torn because they lost a child, so please, spare me your bullshit reasoning."

"You know what Qortni? I didn't call you over here to argue with you, I called you so we could clear any bad air and it seems as if shit is just spiraling out of control..."

She interrupted me in mid thought and said, "Nothing is spiraling out of control but your damn mouth, but it's cool, because Amberlin is definitely showing her true colors, she's thinking about herself and herself only. You either really don't realize how bad your words hurt or you do know and just really don't care and will say whatever comes to mind, but you know what, it's all good. Amber can keep doing what makes her happy and not worry about Qortni and trust and believe I won't worry about you, I'll do what makes me happy and stay out of your life, I'm gone."

Qortni took me totally by surprise and being that I've known my cousin for the length of time we've both been alive, I had to take a couple of steps back and look at myself after she left and I had to reevaluate myself and see if the things she was saying to me rang true, had I changed that much? Was I really happy that Qortni lost her baby?

Was a part of me jealous of her? It was time to start looking at the woman in the mirror...

Qortni

I really didn't mean to go off on Amber the way I had but I really couldn't hold back the feelings that were stirring up in my heart, so I let loose on her. I will admit one thing though, she said something that rang true to me, I think I have used Jaison as my rebound guy. He's been giving me something I have been wanting for the longest, a sense of importance, he made me feel wanted, we enjoyed each other's company without me feeling like I'm not really wanted there. When he and I had conversations he really listened to me and responded to my comments and questions, he made me feel special, something Qamar never really took the time to do, he would do small things, but he never took the time out to make me feel special. When Qamar and I would have a conversation, and certain topics would come up, he would either lie to me to avoid the comment or question or he would straight ignore me. Jaison was almost too good to be true, and I was really starting to have second thoughts about him and I sleeping together, but before I talked to him about my feelings, I for some reason, decided to give Qamar a call to see if he would meet me to talk, I wanted him to hear my side of the story, the full story, and then it would be the both of our decisions to decide if we wanted to try one more time at making this relationship, or lack thereof work, I honestly didn't know what was coming over me, wait, I take that back, I really felt sorry for him, so I decided to give him another chance with me to build his confidence up.

"Qamar, it's Qortni, would you mind meeting me at Starbuck's in Woodbridge?"

"Sure, I'll get my aunt's car and be there in no time, are you alright?"

"Yes, I'm fine, I just think we need to talk and iron some things out, that's all. I mean, if you're busy, then we can meet at a later date."

"Oh, nah, today is cool, I'll be there shortly."

"Okay, see you soon."

"Qortni, before you hang up, I just want to tell you thank you for even considering talking to me, I know you didn't have to call me today, but the fact that you did really touches my heart, and for that, thank you."

"No problem, see you in a few," I responded to him.

"Now that I'm meeting Q in a few, I need to call Jaison and meet up with him tonight so I can tell him we need to stop doing what we're doing, on second thought, I may need to wait until after Qamar and I talk so I can know if Jaison and I really need to stop doing what we're doing," I said aloud to myself while driving to meet Qamar.

Once I finally made it to Starbuck's Qamar was already there and seated waiting on me.

"Hey babe, glad you called me to meet and speak with you," he stood and tried to kiss me on my lips, I turned my face so he could kiss my cheek.

"No problem Qamar, I really called you so I could get some things up off my chest, some things that we may possibly be able to work through and salvage our relationship, or lack thereof."

"That's fine by me, I'm all ears and I'm willing to try and or change anything I may need to change and try in order to get you back, this time without you have been crazy for me, I miss you so much," he told me.

Just as I was about to respond to him, his phone vibrated altering him that he had a text message, and me being me, I peeped the name on the screen from who the message was from, it was from this bird bitch by the name of Durriyah, one of his best friends home girl and a coworker of his that I wasn't too fond of, and I'm sure the feeling was mutual on her end.

"Go ahead and answer her message 'cause if you don't, you already know she's going to either message you again or call you, so go ahead."

"She's not important to me you are, so she'll have to wait."

"I didn't know you were back in contact with her, that must have happened recently. Anyway, I'll patiently wait while you respond to her," I told him while taking my phone out to text Jaison.

"Ok, now that I have responded to her message, we can get to what you want to get off your chest, I'm all ears."

See how he just avoided my comment about that bitch? I'm not going to say any more about it now, I'm going to store that shit in my mental diary and save it, just like he does to me with some things.

"Okay, so the way things ended on Valentine's evening wasn't right at all, but in my defense, the room you got for us to sleep in that night was straight foul and you can't sit there and tell me with a straight face that it wasn't, I mean really? The Regal Inn? Not for nothing, we could have bypassed dinner at Ruth's Chris and went to Friday's or Chili's and you could have a gotten a room at the Marriott or Best Western. When I walked into the Regal Inn that evening, I felt like a cheap whore, not like the woman you claim you love. Like, really though, in all seriousness, what the fuck was going through your mind when you went and reserved that room? I would absolutely love to know."

"Qortni, I admit, I didn't think everything through, and I have to be honest, one of the people that decorated the room for me while we were at dinner told me you wouldn't approve of the room, but against my better judgment and without listening to her, I just kept the room, and for that I apologize."

"Who is 'her' I know you didn't have that slut Durriyah decorate any room for me? Are you fucking kidding me? You know that bitch and me don't get along, why would you even do some shit like that? You are totally bugged out."

"Qortni, Durriyah and I are friends, you're either going to accept that or you can kick rocks, I mean damn, let me find out you're jealous of her?"

"Jealous of that STD infested slut, Negro please, you must have me fucked up with the next bitch, me? Jealous? Never that; you need to recognize who you're talking to."

"Qortni, you get on my nerves you do know that right? But I can't even front, even though you irk me, I still love you and I'll do anything to make you happy and please you even if that means dismissing Durriyah from my circle, then so be it."

"I don't believe you, call her on the phone right now, put her on speaker phone and tell her that you can no longer continue your friendship with her."

"You don't trust me now? What kind of elementary school shit is that?"

"When have I ever fully trusted you? Are you going to do it or not, 'cause if not, I'm out and you can make sure to lose my number and everything else you may have that is associated with me, real shit."

"Fine Qort, have it your way," he responded while calling Durriyah on the phone and telling her that he could no longer be friends with her. It wasn't their friendship that I didn't like, it was the fact that whenever I was in her presence with Qamar I got the weird vibe that the both of them had either fucked or they had planned on fucking, but have Qamar tell it, they're just friends and he doesn't find her attractive. A woman's intuition never fails her, and my gut was telling me that if it hasn't already happened, Qamar and Durriyah will end up fucking. As much as I hate to admit it, she will probably be the reason Qamar and I don't make it.

"Qort, let me ask you something, and I want you to be completely honest with me, do you see us being together in the long run? I'm only asking because I don't want to lose you but at the same time I don't want to waste my time or yours trying to make something work that's not going to work."

"I have mixed emotions about all of this Qamar, I'm going to be honest with you, I don't know what our future holds, I'm not a psychic but I do think we can make this work if we keep our problems limited to the two of us instead of telling everyone and their mama about them, certain friendships on your side or mine need to come to a halt, for the health of this relationship. Now you and I both know there are some female friends on your end that can't stand me for anything, and it's not because of anything I've done, they don't care for me because I'm with you. Now, I don't know if they have feelings that stem deeper than a friendship for you because I don't know, I just know that the last time a female friend of yours had feelings for you that were more of a friendship led to us breaking up cause the bitch lied on me."

"I hear all that you're saying Qort, and I'm going to take all of that into consideration, I swear I am. Now, I have a question, are you willing to give up your friendships with your college friends for the health of our relationship?"

"Before I answer that, let me ask you a question, what male friends of mine do you have problems with? Which one of them disrespects you and our relationship?"

"None of them, matter of fact, I don't even know any of them, met some of them only one time when we went to see Charlie Murphy perform at the college, in other words, point taken."

"Thank you for seeing things my way, not that I would have had a problem doing so, but there's no problem between you and my college friends so there's no real point in me dismissing my friendship with them because of our relationship, they fully respect my relationship with you."

"Fair enough, now are we on one accord now? Can we please move forward and start trying to make this relationship work again?"

"Yes, I don't see why not."

"Cool, we can go bowling tonight if you like? Then we can go to dinner and get a room to celebrate, and no, not the Regal Inn, we can go to a better hotel."

"Sounds like a plan to me, I'll meet you at the bowling alley tonight around nine okay?"

"Why can't I just pick you up? I mean if that's not pushing my limits with you."

"I have some errands to run first then I need to go home and shower, my parents aren't fond of you, not that they were before, but they're borderline hating you after I had my miscarriage, and they don't want you anywhere near the house so I'm just going to meet you at the alley tonight, I'll leave my car there and we can ride to dinner and the hotel together, deal?"

"That's cool with me, I'll see you tonight," he told me while reaching in for a kiss.

After leaving Starbuck's with Qamar, I called Jaison and asked him if there was somewhere we could meet to talk, going to his house was out of the question, simply because I knew that if I were to go to his house to talk, we'd end up fucking and even though his dick was great, I couldn't chance fucking him again and catching even more feelings for him, because Qamar and I were officially back together. We decided to meet at East Rock Park so we could talk, I liked going up there to clear my mind, the scenery was so relaxing, it was therapy for me.

About fifteen minutes after I got up to the top of the mountain I spotted Jaison's Expedition pulling up two parking spaces away from mine. I got out of my car and walked over to the benches that allowed us to view the City of New Haven, Jaison came and joined me on the bench.

"What's going on sweetie? Everything all right, over the phone you sounded as if something is bothering you?"

"Yes and no, I don't really know where to begin, so I guess I just need to speak what's on my heart. On Valentine's evening when I called you to pick me up, I should have went with my gut instinct and just stayed at my cousin's house like I had planned to, I messed up by staying at your house and by sleeping with you. Don't get me wrong, I love the time that we have spent together and the sexual chemistry we have, but I think I may have started catching feelings for you way too soon, you were sort of like my rebound guy and I don't want to hurt you. Qamar and I are going to give our relationship one last chance, I don't know what's going to happen between the both of us, but I do know that he does love me and maybe somewhere down the line I'll learn how to love him. I said all of that to say this, I hope being that we were friends before we became intimate with one another, we can continue to remain friends, hang out from time to time, and just continue to be cool."

"I can't knock you at all for your decision, I mean I kind of saw it coming, and please don't take any offense to what I'm about to say to you, you know you're a beautiful young lady Qort, you don't need the bullshit that comes with being with him, you can do a lot better, you just need to look deep down into your soul to see how all these other guys out here and I see you. You can do so much better than being with a boy who calls himself a man but puts his hands on women like a punk. I'm going to always be here for you Qortni, trust and believe that, I'm just a phone call away I have your back a hundred grand," he told me then kissed me on my cheek.

"You do know that if he and I didn't get back together you and I would have ended up being a couple right?"

"Is that so? You're so sure of yourself aren't you?"

"I'm just stating facts, you don't agree?"

"I'm pleading the fifth on that one, care to go out for a friendly drink tonight?" he responded changing the subject.

"I so wish I could, but Qamar and I are going out tonight, and as a matter of fact, I need to go finish running some errands and to take my shower so I can get dressed."

"Fair enough, mama, just hit me up whenever you need to talk or want to go out, I'll be around," he told me as he headed to his ride.

I felt so terrible, as Jaison walked away I felt like a piece of me was walking away, I definitely know I caught feelings for him way too soon, but shit, what's done is done.

A month later

Qamar and I have been back together officially for a month and so far so good, but it's still early in the game so it's too early to call things perfect. I've spoken to Jaison a couple of times since I told him Qamar and I were going to try to make things work. I've tried to meet up with him for drinks a couple of times, but he's always been busy or had something planned already, no sweat.

Amberlin and I have gotten back on good terms and I'm elated about that, she's my bitch for life, my favorite cousin, and my best friend. I started a new job, which is more money and which will help me stack my bread so I can get my own ride, bumming rides, walking and borrowing other people's cars is getting to be a bit much, especially with the people in my family, who can be downright stingy when it comes to letting me drive their car. When I got hired for this new job, I had no clue that Qamar had also applied for the same job, same shift, not the best decision, especially if that means we'll be working together.

"So, how do you feel about us working together Qort? I think it'll be a good look, we can ride into work together, and after work we can spend some time together before you have to go to your second job."

"I'm honestly not feeling the idea of us working together, I mean really? All that time together at work for eight hours, then you want me to come home with you at your grandmother's house after work to lay up with you? That's a bit much, too much time with each other isn't going to be good for us, we're going to get tired of one another before we know it, and we all know that it's going to lead to arguments, and us breaking up, and I already told you this last time was the last time we were going to get back together after breaking up with one another. I don't see any good coming out of us working with one another; I'm just keeping it a buck."

"Think positive thoughts baby, positive thoughts, we'll be fine, nothing and no one at the job will come between what you and I have, trust me on that one, you have my word."

"You can think positively all you want Qamar, I'm thinking realistically, but have it your way, you'll see, nothing good is going to come out of this as far as our relationship is concerned, you can mark my words."

Two weeks into working the new job, and so far everything is cool with Qamar and I working at the same place, even though he's a little upset that I refuse to ride into work with him, I'm just not trying to be up under him that long, I mean I understand he's trying to make an effort to show me that he wants our relationship to work, but damn, I need some breathing space.

I have become cool with two females that I work with, Quetta and Shanique; they seem to be pretty cool. Shanique went to high school with my brother and I; she lives around the corner from me, and Quetta, I've never seen a day in my life, but she seems to be pretty cool, the three of us kind of formed a little clique pretty quickly. There were two young chicks that worked with us on the graveyard shift and one of them I know because she went to high school with me, I think she's like a year or two behind me. Anyhow, she and her homegirl are nothing but sluts, her homegirl has run through almost any and all desperate men in all of the hoods in New Haven, and there are quite a few hoods. Anyhow, I have noticed Qamar always having his eyes on that slut's ass, and I'm not knocking him for looking, I mean he is a man and men do have eyes, but shit, don't make that shit so obvious. Everyone at the job notices it, like what the fuck is that all about? One night while at work, I decided to approach him on it on one of our breaks, I wasn't about to let this shit ride until we got off.

"So, I see you can't seem to get any work done tonight because you're too busy watching Taja's ass, what the fuck is that all about?"

"Qort, what the fuck are you talking about?" he asked me with his head hanging low.

"You know exactly what I'm talking about, your eyes planted on Taja's ass since she fucking walked into the store tonight, and I ask again, what the fuck is that all about?"

One thing I knew about Qamar was that when he was lying or caught in a lie he would always hang his head low and would avoid all eye contact with me.

"Qortni, really? All of this shit is in your head, why would I do that knowing we work together? That's just not smart on my end, I'm not that stupid."

"Yes really Qamar, everyone in here has noticed it, not just me, so please quit your bullshitting and just own up to it, man the hell up!"

"Fine, yes, I've copped a couple of looks at her ass, but I'm a man what do you expect?"

"It wasn't a couple of times Qamar, you've been looking at her ass all night, even subconsciously grabbed ya dick a couple of times while you were staring at it, straight disrespecting!"

"Qort, can we continue this conversation after we get off work when we're alone? This is not the time or the place to be having this convo."

"Nah, I'm finishing this convo right now, you didn't wait until we were alone to look and think about that bitch's ass, so I'm not going to wait to approach you about it. Do you want to fuck that slut?"

"I'm not having this conversation with you right now Qortni, I'll continue this when we get off tonight," he told me while getting up and walking back to the main store.

"I can't believe this lying, little dick bastard!" I said to myself aloud.

"Qort, you alright? I heard you and Qamar going at it," Quetta asked me.

"Yeah girl I'm alright, he just doesn't know how to keep his eyes to himself. He doesn't know how to be discreet about his shit, I don't mind him looking, but when he starts looking at another female's ass then start grabbing his dick as if he's fantasizing about fucking this broad it's a damn problem."

"You need to handle that, and fast before he tries to fuck her."

"In all seriousness, I want him to fuck her. As a matter of fact, I'm going to give him the green light to fuck her, just to get it out of his system."

"You're crazy, what happens if he really does fuck her? You'll be mad as hell then, don't go offering him something if you don't really want him to go through with it, that's dangerous."

"At this point in time, I don't even care; all the shit he and I have been through in the past couple of years, I can't deal anymore. When we get off in the morning I'm going to tell him since he fantasizes about her ass, he might as well go fuck the bitch."

"So, I'm going to ask you one more time, do you want to fuck that broad Taja?"

"Yes, I do want to fuck her."

His words hit me like a ton of bricks and I stopped my car in the middle of the street. I looked at him, pulled my car into the cemetery and told his ass to get the fuck out of my car.

"Qort, can we talk about this please? You asked me a question and instead of me lying, I told you the truth, would you rather have me lie to you?"

"I don't want to be bothered any more Qamar, call that bitch and tell her to come pick you up since you want to fuck her. I do appreciate you telling me the truth, but damn. How would you feel if every time I say a man I wanted to fuck I all of a sudden start fingering myself? How would that make you feel?

"It would make me feel less of a man, make me feel like I just don' do it for you any more."

"Exactly, now do us both a favor and leave me alone, don't bother calling me."

"Before you pull off Qortni, let me at least get my things out of your car, you know my CD player and my CD's please."

I didn't even respond, I simply rolled the passenger side window down and threw all of his things out of my car, making certain his CD player broke into pieces.

"Qortni, it's cold as hell out here and it's raining, can you at least bring me home?"

I laughed at him and looked at him like he was crazy, I responded, "You must be crazy, tell that hoe to come get you and bring you home."

It started to rain hard and I wasn't feeling sorry for him nor the fact that he was going to have to walk about two miles home from the cemetery where I kicked him out of my car. I had had enough of his bullshit, I was tired of all of his shit, and I had officially had enough. As I was leaving the cemetery my boy from both of my jobs pulled up into the cemetery, I guess Qamar had called him to give him a ride home because it was raining so hard out.

Q amar and my boy Sheadon have been blowing up my phone all day long and I was getting tired of them both. I mean really? Between the both of them my phone must have rang about seventy times today and I was getting aggravated to the max. The last time Sheadon called me I decided to answer to see what he wanted, even though I already know he's going to try to defuse the situation between Qamar and me.

"Qortni, that's how we do? You ignore my phone calls? You must have forgotten that I'm not ya man Qamar."

"I didn't forget but I know you're calling me to talk to me about him and I don't want to talk to him or about him, I'm good on him, he has no type of respect for me or for our relationship, I'm not around for that shit any longer."

"I feel you, but shit, he was over here at my crib for like six hours the other day drinking and professing his love for you, he knows he fucked up, and he's sorry, give that man another chance, you know you love him Q."

"You must not have gotten the memo, I don't love him, I like him, yes, but love him, no I haven't gotten that far yet, and if he loved me and respected our relationship, the bullshit that came out of his mouth about him wanting to fuck Taja would have never came out, some things are better left in your head."

"Just give it some thought, I told him to give you a little time to cool down and to stop calling or texting you, he's very sorry Q, give him one last chance."

"I'm not around for that anymore. I'm good, I rather be pissed and lonely than to be pissed and in a relationship, especially with his bitch ass. He really thinks he's doing me a favor by being my man, but in fact, I'm doing his ass a favor by being his woman. Do you realize how many men are waiting for me to drop him so they can show me how a woman

121

is supposed to be treated? I'm good, I'm going to get myself together and move on."

"Aight Qort, have it your way; you going to be at the college tomorrow working? I'm going to swing by and see you."

"Yeah I'll be there, I'm leaving the second job a little earlier so I can be there on time, I'm glad it's only four hours tomorrow, both of these jobs are kicking my ass."

"I feel you, I'll see you tomorrow then, I'll holla."

After getting off the phone with Sheadon, I decided to take about an hour nap before I had to get up and start getting ready for work, as soon as my head hit the pillow my phone began ringing, it was nobody but Qamar so I ignored the call and went to sleep.

When I got dressed and headed outside to my car so I could be on my way to work, Qamar was sitting on the hood of my car, no telling how long he was out there.

"Qamar, what are you doing at my house and why the hell are you sitting on the hood of my new car? Have you officially lost your mind?"

"No I haven't lost my mind, but I came over here so we could talk before we go to work tonight, I tried calling you but you didn't answer, so I figured there was no better way for me to get your attention than to show up at your house, you have no choice but to hear me out now."

I walked over to my car, got in and started the ignition. I let my driver's side window down and told him, "I advise you to get up off my car before I run you over when I pull off."

"You're not going to do that to me Qortni, you love me too much."

"Try me, now please get off my car Qamar, this is going to be the last time I ask you, before I put my car in drive and drive off with you on my car."

"I'm not getting off until you talk to me."

"I'm not going to be late for work because you want to play these stupid ass games tonight, I don't have time for this shit. Now I'm pulling off."

I put my car in drive and pulled off with Qamar on my hood, and once I got passed the light that was at my corner, I increased my speed until he fell off, and it felt damn good not to care whether or not he was hurt, he should have gotten off when I first told him to.

Three hours later at work

"Qortni, did you really drive off with Qamar sitting on the hood of your car?" Quetta asked me.

"I absolutely did, I told him to get off, he wasn't trying to hear me so I pulled off, I wasn't about to be late playing with his ass, I'm not around for that shit; wait, how did you know?"

"You're crazy, he's over there telling all the guys about how sore he is and they asked him what happened, you know I'm nosey so I was listening to their conversation," she told me laughing so hard to the point she was crying.

"That's exactly what he gets; no one has time to play with him when money is on their mind."

"I knew there was a reason I liked you, you and I think alike, good shit," Quetta told me.

The rest of the night went without incident and surprisingly Qamar didn't try to engage in any type of conversation with me. As our third shift crew was leaving for the night, Quetta, Shanique and I made plans to go to the concert that was a few weeks away in lieu of my birthday, and boy when Qamar overheard our conversation he was pissed to say the least.

"Qort, I have something planned for your birthday and you're over here making plans to go out with your girls?"

"Sure am, I didn't know about any plans for my birthday, I want to go to this concert and I want to be stress free that night, so I'm going with my girls, got a problem with that?"

"Yeah I do, so can you please cancel your plans? I really put a lot of work into making your birthday special for you, something you will never forget."

"Qort, we can go to the concert in New York the week after your birthday, go ahead and rock out with Qamar for your birthday, New York will be a lot more fun than going to Hartford, trust," Quetta told me, but I wasn't trying to hear it.

"You sure Quetta? I mean I really have my heart set on going to that concert since it's the night of my birthday."

Quetta pulled me to the side so Qamar couldn't hear our conversation, "Qort, stop being a bitch towards that man, go ahead and rock out with him and his plans for your birthday, he looked hurt when he heard our plans, don't do that to him, we will have a lot more fun in New York, so much more to do in New York and we can probably stay over, and do some sightseeing while we're out there."

"Aight, I'll rock out with him for my birthday, then the three of us will rock out in New York for the weekend, fair enough."

"Qamar, I'll go through with your plans for my birthday, and I'm telling you now, you better have put your best foot forward and I better not regret cancelling this concert for you."

Now, I know y'all are asking yourselves "why is this dumb chick agreeing to go out with him for her birthday and she just knocked him off of her car and she kicked him out of her car not too long ago when he told her he wanted to screw one of their co-workers? I'm agreeing to go out with him because I want to see if he has stepped his game up since Valentine's Day.

My birthday evening

I called Amberlin to do my hair for me in preparation for my evening with Qamar for my birthday. I decided to rock a pink BabyPhat dress that was open in the front, enough material only to cover my breasts, and I had some six inch cream colored heels from my friend's boutique to go with the dress, I was dressed to kill tonight.

"Damn chick, that dress is bad, you're sure to get a rise out of Qamar and whomever else is around y'all tonight."

"Thank you mama, I treated myself as an early birthday gift, I got this dress on sale before Kimora merged her website with Macy's, as soon as I laid eyes on it I knew I had to have it."

"I may have to borrow that from you one day; that dress is fierce. Has Qamar told you what the plans are for this evening?"

"No, he hasn't said anything to me, I think he's still pissed that I initially made plans to go to the concert tonight instead of going out with him, I just don't want to be stressed tonight and I don't want to end up being disappointed. I mean you and I both know that he's the king of disappointment on special occasions."

"I know mama, but hope and pray for the best and I'm going to pray that he got it right because I know if he didn't you're going to kick his ass."

"I feel bad Amber."

"Why? Feel bad about what?"

"I feel bad because I only agreed to go out with him tonight because I'm secretly hoping that he does fuck up just so I can have a valid reason to not deal with him any longer, I'm tired of acting like I'm happy with him and this relationship, or shall I say lack thereof. I want out, but no matter how hard I try to leave he just won't let me be."

"Just end it and move on already, no sense in hanging on to something that isn't going anywhere. You're wasting your time if you think things are going to get better, y'all have been through hell enough times already in the two years you've been together and honestly, I can't ever remember a time where he made you happy or when you weren't upset or angry at him, count your blessings as you cut your losses with him, move on girl."

I let Amberlin's words sink in, and I thought about what Nathan told me the day I had my miscarriage, when he told me I could do a lot better than being with Qamar and that I need not let Qamar break me down and it seems as if he's been doing a lot of that lately. He mentioned that I needed to put my foot down and end this relationship before someone gets hurt, physically and emotionally. They both said basically the same thing, and I was really starting to think that they were both right, it was time Qamar and I called it quits.

As soon as Amberlin put the finishing touches on my hair Qamar called me and told me he was five minutes away from my house, so I decided to walk Amber outside to her car and just wait for Qamar out there. As Amber was getting into her car, Jaison called me.

"Hey stranger, how are you?"

"Hey love, I'm good, I was just calling you to wish you a very happy birthday. You know I couldn't let the night end without wishing you a happy birthday; that would be inconsiderate."

"Aww, thank you sweetie, I definitely appreciate it. I honestly thought you had forgotten my birthday, seeing that it has been a while since we've talked, I thought you forgot about me."

"I can never forget about you Qortni, I just wanted to give you your space and respect your relationship with that other dude, I didn't want to cause any trouble between the both of you, so I decided to keep my distance."

"I respect it, and I appreciate your respect for the relationship. I miss you Jaison, I miss us, what we shared, the fun times we had, even if it was only a short time, I miss the way you make me feel."

"How do I make you feel Qort?"

"You make me feel wanted, like you enjoy my company, like you only have eyes for me when we're together."

"Qort, I want to see you tonight, can you make that happen?"

As I was about to answer him, Qamar was pulling up.

"Jaison, I have to go, let's link up tomorrow, Qamar is taking me out tonight and he just pulled up and I can't renege, I'll call you tomorrow."

"I'll be looking forward to hearing from you. Love you Qortni."

Jaison telling me he loved me definitely threw me for a loop; that was definitely something I was not expecting, he now had my mind thinking a mile a minute.

Qamar got out of the car, came around to the passenger side and opened my door, that was a huge shock in itself. In our two years of dating, this is the first time ever that he has opened any door for me, kudos to him for that. Now just to hope the rest of the evening goes without a problem.

"You look nice Qortni, that dress is definitely doing some things for me."

"Thank you, I appreciate it."

"Are you alright? You seem to be preoccupied with your thoughts, is everything okay?"

"Everything is fine Qamar, what's on the agenda for tonight?"

"Well, we're going to start out with dinner at Chili's, then we're going to take in a sightseeing cruise in New York, followed by a room at the Stamford Marriott Hotel that was decorated by me, and ending tomorrow morning with breakfast in bed; I promise you're going to absolutely enjoy yourself tonight."

"Sounds promising," I responded dryly.

"Qort, something is bothering you, I can tell, you're not your normal self, you don't even seem as if you're interested in going out with me tonight for your birthday. What's going on with you? What thoughts are preoccupying your mind right now?"

"Do you see the both of us together in the next one to five years?"

"Whoa, where did that come from?"

"Answer the question Qamar, and answer truthfully."

"I honestly don't know Qort; I mean I would love for us to be together a year, five years, even fifty years from now, but who knows? I don't know the future, we just have to take this relationship a day at a time and whatever happens; happens."

"Okay, fair enough."

The conversation I had with Jaison had me really thinking and it made me wonder if I honestly made the mistake of getting back with Qamar. I mean what if everything that happened on Valentine's Day when Qamar and I broke up was supposed to happen so Jaison and I could be together? My thoughts were getting the best of me right now and I felt bad because Qamar was probably feeling like I didn't want to be bothered with him tonight. Why did Jaison have to tell me that he loved me? I was beginning to second; third and fourth guess my decision to stay with Qamar.

"If you don't want to go out tonight for your birthday, let me know, we can just go to the room and chill for the whole evening, or I can bring you back home, the decision is yours."

"Hell no, you damn near threw a temper tantrum because you had all of this planned when I wanted to go to the concert tonight, oh trust, we're going to do everything you have planned for tonight."

He smiled and said, "Great to hear, I can't wait until you see the room I got for you, I think you're really going to love it."

"I can't wait."

Once we got to the restaurant, the waitress seated us immediately. Being that Amber and I popped a couple of bottles of wine earlier at my house I was in dire need of the ladies room.

"I'll be right back, I need to go to the restroom, but if the waitress comes back for the drink orders, can you order me the Tropical Sunrise Margarita please?"

"Yea, I got you."

As I was making my way to the restroom, my heart dropped at what I saw or rather whom I saw at a corner table in the restaurant.

I went to the bathroom and just let the tears flow freely from my face, I didn't even care about messing up my makeup, and my heart was torn. After about five minutes, I composed myself and joined Qamar back at the table.

"Everything alright Qortni? Your face looks like you've been crying."

"I'm good sweetie, trust me, I'm good, no worries, let's enjoy our night."

"Cool, the best answer I've heard from you all night long."

After Qamar and I enjoyed our dinner, we headed to New York to enjoy the sightseeing cruise he set up for me, and boy was I enjoying myself, a little more than I really wanted to. He definitely put his best foot forward; he was finally showing me that he cared.

"Qamar, this cruise is awesome, you know I've been to New York countless times but I've never been sightseeing, this is absolutely beautiful, thank you for a wonderful night so far," I told him while leaning in to kiss him.

"You're welcome Qortni. I know we've had a hell of a lot of ups and downs in our relationship, but I want you to know that I absolutely love you and I apologize for anything and everything that I may have either said or done to disrespect you or our relationship or to make you feel as if you're not important to me, because you are my world."

He made me cry and I absolutely hate showing emotions, but he brought it out of me tonight. I felt like such a punk crying in front of him and I felt even worse because I knew that this feeling would only last until he pissed me off, and I knew that moment was coming sooner or later, kind of negative but true.

After the cruise we headed to Stamford to the Marriott hotel and just from the entrance of the hotel, I could tell that Qamar pulled out all the stops, this hotel was absolutely gorgeous, and he definitely made up for that bullshit ass hotel on that Valentine's Day.

When we got outside of our room, he blindfolded me, opened the door and helped me into the room. Once we got into the room he took my blindfold off and to say I was speechless was definitely an understatement, the room was absolutely amazing, he decorated the room in my favorite colors, blue and white. The Jacuzzi in the room had blue and white rose petals floating around, the tub in the bathroom was surrounded by blue and white tea light candles, there were blue and white rose petals on the floor going from the door in the room to the bathroom and surrounding the bed, along with a message that spelled happy birthday Qort, he had definitely outdid himself.

"Qamar, this is absolutely breathtaking, I can't believe you did all of this for me," I told him getting choked up.

"Why wouldn't I do all of this for you? You absolutely deserve it, it's your day, nothing but the best for you," he told me embracing me in a hug from the back.

"I mean I have been acting like a total bitch to you since I had my miscarriage, I don't deserve all of this."

"Yes you do, that's why I did it for you, and the fact that I caused you to suffer the miscarriage. I beat myself up every day because we would be parents now, enjoying our child, and no doubt we'd both be a lot happier. All of this right here is a birthday slash Valentine's Day slash I know I fucked up type thing, I just want you to enjoy yourself tonight."

I couldn't hold the tears back any longer, thoughts and memories of the day I had my miscarriage still stung like it was only a few days ago, I will never forget that day, I still have my baby's ultrasound pictures in frames that are standing on my dresser.

Qamar helped me undress and we both got into the Jacuzzi, and we made love, well, his version of making love to me, but I promised myself I wasn't going to complain about his sex tonight because even though he lacked in the sex department, he definitely made up for it with everything he did for me tonight, from dinner to the cruise and the room, I was in heaven.

The next morning

Last night was epic, Qamar and I must have fucked about fifteen times everywhere in the room that would hold us, and I had to soak in the tub this morning before getting dressed because my pussy was so sore and swollen. Before checking out of the hotel, he had breakfast served to me while I was still in bed, it was phenomenal. Truth be told, I wasn't ready for my birthday weekend to end, but I knew it had to, so after sexing me like three more times Qamar and I both packed our bags, got showered and dressed and checked out of the hotel. Even though I had the best time in our relationship last night with Qamar, my thoughts started drifting off to what Jaison told me last night over the phone. I pulled my phone out and decided to text him.

"Hey Jaison, I'm on my way back in town but before we meet up I wanted to let you know that you definitely threw me for a loop last night when you told me you loved me, I was totally caught off guard. I don't know how to take that comment, I'm still trying to figure that one out, and I'll be looking for some clarity when we meet up later on today. ~Qortni."

He replied with the quickness, "You will definitely have some clarity once we link up today, I meant every word I said, I can't wait to see you, call me when you're on your way here, I know you need play by play direction on how to get here, LOL."

I smiled to hold the tears back that were dying to slide down my face.

"What got you smiling over there? I haven't seen you smile this much in a long time, except for yesterday."

"It's nothing."

"Qortni, it is something, you're over there smiling extra hard, now what it is, or shall I say who is it?"

132

"Qamar, leave it alone please, I'm not about to start with you this morning, I'm not in the mood for it so please just leave it alone."

He pulled over in the breakdown lane on the highway and put the car in park.

"Qortni, I'm not playing with you and I'm not trying to argue with you, I simply asked you a question, now who are you texting that has you smiling so much?" he asked reaching for my phone.

He knew one thing I hated the most was for him to grab my phone, my phone was my business; I never tried to take his phone out of his hands so had better chill.

"Qamar, can you take me home please? I have things to do today, Quetta, Shanique and I are going shopping for the concert, I'm not trying to be late because you want to be up all in my business, now it's none of your concern who is on my phone with me texting, now let's go please," I told him while putting my phone in my bag and laying my seat back, I was starting to get a headache and I needed to shake it before the girls and I went shopping.

"Have it your way Qortni, but I swear to God if I find out you're cheating on me I'm going to whoop your ass, believe that," he told me then pulled back on to the highway.

"Qamar, your threats don't faze me, I wish you would put your hands on me again, I swear the next time you put your hands on me you won't live to see another day."

He looked at me like I was crazy, probably because I never came at him like that and I never threatened him before, but I was tired of his bullshit. I meant every word I said to him, I would try my best to kill him the next time he decided to put his hands on me; I was tired of being his human punching bag.

He side eyed me and smirked before saying, "Qort, you don't have the heart to harm me, deep down you know you love me, so please stop acting like you're tough because we both know you're not."

"For as long as we have been together, you definitely don't know me, but trust, the next time you put your hands on me you will see me in a way you have never seen me before, try me if you like. I take a lot of shit from you Qamar and I'm done doing that, you have cheated on me countless times and I'm done acting like the shit doesn't affect me, just try me Qamar, I'm hoping you fuck up one more time just so you can see how it feels to get fucked up."

"Aight, Qortni, I'll leave you be, but please don't fuck around and slip up and allow me to catch you cheating because I'm telling you now, it won't be a good look for you nor for the guy your caught with, that's my word because if I cant have you, no one else can either, and that's my word."

I can't lie, when he said if he couldn't have me then no one else could kind of scared me because it meant that he would do whatever was in his power to keep me to himself and make sure no one else got close to me, I honestly don't know if I was supposed to feel flattered or threatened, it was kind of scary. Instead of responding to his threat I simply laid my head back on the headrest, put my sunglasses on and tuned him out.

Once we got back into town I called Amber to fill her in on the events of my birthday night, then I called Quetta and Shanique to we could meet up and go shopping for outfits for the concert in New York, Amber decided to join us and make this a birthday shopping spree for me and a ladies day out that would ultimately extend into a ladies night out.

"So Qort how was your birthday yesterday? I see you didn't kill Qamar so things must have been pretty good," Quetta said to me.

"Things were great until we got in the car this morning and I started texting a friend of mine, Qamar damn near blew a fuse because I was smiling at my text messages, he wanted to know who I was texting, who else besides him I was fucking, he was just acting like a jealous little bitch in the car coming back into town."

"Did you tell him who you were texting? Matter of fact who were you texting? Let me find out you have a new boo on the low," Shanique said.

"Nah, no new boo on the low, I was texting my boy Jaison because he called me out of the blue yesterday just as Qamar was pulling up to get me, and he told me he loved me which totally took me by surprise, I was telling him that I was going to link up with him today so we could talk, we haven't really spoken since Qamar and I got back together and I needed some clarity as to how or why he loves me being that we haven't spoken or seen each other in quite some time."

"How come we haven't met this mystery friend of yours?" Quetta asked me.

"He's been a friend of mine for at least two years, he likes to keep a low profile, he doesn't really go out that much, he's basically a homebody, maybe all of you will meet one day, who knows."

"You say he's just a friend, but I can bet you any amount of money that he's a friend with many benefits isn't he?" Shanique asked laughing.

"No longer friends with benefits, just straight friends, he respects the relationship Qamar and I have and he only called me last night to wish me a happy birthday," I told all three of them, I was getting tired of playing twenty one questions with them today.

After we spent a good four hours in the mall, we parted ways and decided to all meet up at Shanique's house in about four hours so we could all take pictures before heading out for the evening to continue celebrating my birthday.

After leaving the girls, I called Jaison up to see if he was busy, he and I had a lot to talk about and I wanted to talk to him before I stepped out with my girls tonight. He gave me directions to his house and when I got there he looked as if he was overly excited to see me.

"You know I've been missing you right?" he asked me as he embraced me in a tight hug as soon as he opened his front door.

"Really?" I responded with my eyebrows arched.

"Hell yea I've missed you, you haven't missed me?"

"I've missed you a little bit."

"I think you've missed me a lot but you just don't want to admit it, do you want anything to eat or drink? You know I have some wine in the basement."

"I'll take a bottle of water if you have it, thank you."

"Are you alright? You seem as if something is bothering you."

"Did you mean what you said last night over the phone about you loving me?"

"Of course I did, I do love you, why would I lie about something like that?"

"So, do you love me the same way you love the chick you put the ring on last night at Chili's?"

He looked like a deer caught in headlights, his eyes grew big, he responded, "Qortni, I can explain all of that, just hear me out."

"I don't even need to hear you out, I have no reason to be mad, I'm in a relationship, it's cool. You almost had me, but like I said, it's cool, you're not obligated to give me a reason for what you did and said last night, it is what it is," I told him while heading to his front door.

"Qort, can you just let me explain?"

"Explain what Jaison? Explain how you had me sleeping in your house, fucking your brains out, going out with me, all while you had a girl the whole time? Did you kick your girl to the curb for me on that Valentine's evening I asked you to pick me up after Qamar and I had a fight?"

"Qortni, please sit down so we can talk about this, I feel as if I owe you that much. Monica and I just got back together; yes, her and I were having our problems around the same time you and Qamar were having problems as well, when you called me on Valentine's evening, Monica and I had a fight and about an hour before you called she moved all of her things out of my crib. Technically she and I weren't together when I offered you a place to stay that night, I'm not that fucked up to do something like that. Being with you that short period of time confirmed what I had believed since we became friends at work, you're a special female, you deserve the best, from the best and even though I put that ring on her finger last night, I don't love her like I love you, I've fallen in love with you, I love you from my soul Qortni."

"Jaison, if you supposedly love me so much from your soul, then why did you propose to her last night? Why do you feel as if it's okay to play with people's emotions?"

"When you told me you and Qamar had gotten back together I knew then that the possibility of you and I being together was a wrap, it just wasn't going to happen and being that I know how Monica feels about me and her and I have about five years of history, I figured that in time my feelings for her would come around, you totally fucked up my heart by telling me that you decided to give him another chance, especially after all he has put you through since the both of you have been together, I want you as my woman, not only my friend, and if that means breaking off my engagement with Monica then I'll do so, as long as you promise me we'll be together."

I couldn't take too much more of this, I felt as if he was playing with my heart, and my heart was nothing to be played with, it was sensitive.

"Jaison I can't promise you that, but I can tell you that I'm a little disappointed in how things played out, I thought you were better than this, and you played with my emotions, but as I said earlier, I can't really be mad because we are not a couple, we were merely friends with benefits, so go ahead and rock out with Monica, I wish the both of you nothing but happiness," I told him right before leaving him and getting into my car.

I was shocked to say the least, but I was sure to get over it, I mean, Jaison was kind of like the rebound guy for me in my time of need; it is what it is, I guess if I look at things from a clearer perspective, I was his rebound chick, I can't even be mad.

After leaving Jaison's crib, I decided to call Amberlin to let her know I was on my way over there and that I would be getting dressed for our evening events at her place.

"Where are you coming from? It normally doesn't take you this long to get here from your house."

"I stopped by Jaison's house after we all split up earlier, I needed some clarity on him telling me he loved me yesterday over the phone, and I got clarity plus a punch to the heart."

"He put his hands on you?"

"Hell no, he proposed to his girl last night. I saw the whole thing when Qamar and I went out to eat. He and his girl were in the corner of the restaurant and when I was on my way to the bathroom I saw him proposing to her; he said that around the time him and I were chilling and him and his girl were beefing, so I was in essence his rebound girl. He insists that he loves me, and even though I believe him, my heart won't let me do it for fear of being hurt by him in the long run; and don't you dare say 'I told you so' I don't even want to hear it."

"I wasn't going to say that, I was merely going to ask you if you were alright I mean I know how you feel about him, and I don't want to see you hurt or crying over a guy that thought he was going to get over on you."

"That's why I came to you to talk cuz, I mean Shanique and Quetta are cool but I've known you my whole life and I know you'll give me advice straight with no chaser."

"Family always has to stick together cuz, remember that, no matter what I will always have your best interest at heart and I will always have your back."

After Amber and I talked about my relationship issues, she sprung a huge announcement on me, she and Nathan were expecting their first child together and I was so elated! She hadn't told anyone else in the family yet as she was still in the beginning stages of her pregnancy, two months to be exact and she didn't want to jinx anything.

"So, if you're pregnant, we're definitely not going out tonight, you can't drink and I'm not about to have Nathan mad at me for bringing you out with me tonight, how about we do ladies night at my house?"

"It's up to you, it's your birthday weekend, whatever makes your heart happy, but for the record, I don't mind going out and Nathan wouldn't mind either, we can all go out to dinner, do movies, we don't necessarily have to go to a club, but like I said, it's your birthday weekend, it's your call."

"Let me call Quetta and Shanique and let them know the club is out, and before we all head out, we can do each other's makeup, it'll be fun."

"It's a date, I'm about to go get in the shower, and it's going to take me a minute to get ready."

"You're acting like you're already six months pregnant," I told her laughing.

"I'm already slower than I used to be, jerk," she replied laughing as well.

While Amber was in the shower I called Quetta and Shanique on three way and told them the plans have slightly changed, we were going to go out to dinner, then the movies, and then maybe out for ice cream.

Three months later

Ever since Jaison and I stopped speaking, even on a friendly level Qamar and I have been getting along pretty well, Nathan and Amber are quite excited about the bundle of joy they have coming, they're five months into their pregnancy and Qamar and I just found out that we're two months pregnant and I pray to God this pregnancy goes smoothly because I really want to have this baby, Qamar promised me that he wouldn't put his hands on me or do anything to cause me to have a miscarriage like the first time.

Nathan and Amberlin have found out that they're expecting a boy and I can't wait to see and spoil my new little cousin, and I can't wait to see what Qamar and I are going to have because then our child and

Amberlin's son will be able to have play dates, the mere thought of is makes me heart smile.

I was on my way to East Rock Mountain to do some much needed writing, just to clear my thoughts and I got a phone call from Amber, it sounded as if she was crying.

"Hey Qort, are you busy?"

"No, just about to go up to East Rock to do some writing, what's going on? Are you alright, it sounds like you're crying."

"I keep having very bad cramps and I'm bleeding, I need a ride to my doctor's office, can you bring me?"

"No doubt, I'll be there in two minutes."

It normally took me at least ten minutes to get to her house, but the urgency in her voice was telling me that she was scared and that she was in dire need to get to her doctor's office, so I put the pedal to the medal and literally made it to her house in two minutes flat, breaking every city speed law there was.

"Amber, where are you?" I called out after not seeing her in her master bedroom.

"I'm in the small bathroom trying to get dressed! Come help me please," she responded through sobs.

I went to the bathroom where she was and told her to just throw on anything, time was of the essence and we needed to get her to her doctor's office.

Her OB/GYN was at the office door waiting on her, something told me that wasn't a good sign, and I just began to pray that Amber hadn't suffered another miscarriage.

"Amber, tell me what happened again, when did you notice the bleeding?"

"I was on my way to the bathroom to shower and head out to run some errands and I sat on the toilet because I was having some minor cramps that I thought nothing of. I thought I may have had to have a bowel movement, and when I peed, I noticed I was peeing blood. Is everything going to be all right Doc?"

"I'm sending you right over to the hospital, direct admit, they're waiting on you, you're in labor and I want to stop it, which might mean you being on bed rest in the hospital for the next two months or more."

"What do you mean I'm in labor? I'm only five months pregnant? It's way too early for me to be in labor, my baby won't survive if I deliver now, what's going on? Why is this happening to me?"

"Amber come on, we need to get over to the hospital, you can ask more questions when you get settled in over there, let's go, the more time you spend over here asking questions, the less time the doctors have to help save the baby."

"Qort, I don't want to lose my baby, I can't go through another miscarriage, I want this baby, I've been going to all of my appointments, taking my vitamins, doing everything I 'm supposed to do to make sure my baby makes it," she told me crying her eyes out. My heart sank for her, I knew exactly what she was feeling, and I said a silent prayer that the baby could be saved, and that I didn't go through this again.

Once we got to the hospital, they took Amber right up to her room and hooked her up to all types of monitors and put a couple of different IV's in her. I have never seen her look so scared before, the tears in her eyes poured down her face so freely, I couldn't help but cry as well.

Qamar and I were supposed to be going out tonight, but there no was no way in hell I was leaving my cousins' side in her time of need, especially since when I suffered my miscarriage she was there for me from start to finish. I decided to call him to let him know that we would have to reschedule our plans, and to say he was disappointed was an understatement, but it is what it is. I wasn't leaving Amber here by herself. After getting off the phone with Qamar, I called Nathan to let him know that he needed to get over to the hospital as soon as he could; Amber needed all the support she could get.

"Qortni, is my baby going to make it? Be honest with me."

"Honestly Amber, I don't know, but I do know that I've been praying a lot for you lately. I don't want you to have a miscarriage, and if you do deliver early, I pray the baby makes it, and I pray that the doctors do everything in their power to ensure that the baby is healthy."

"I'm going to try to go to sleep now, I have too much on my mind, please don't leave me here by myself, will you stay here with me overnight?"

"Absolutely, I'm going to run down to the café to get something to eat, do you want me to bring you anything? Just some chips and something to drink, anything but soda will be fine, thank you."

"No doubt, I'll be right back up."

As I was leaving her room Nathan was coming in and stopped me right outside of the room to ask how Amber was holding up.

"How is she doing?"

"She's highly emotional, she's scared, she said she's going to try to take a nap because she's tired and she wants to de-stress a little bit, she's been crying since she was on the phone with me earlier today," I told him as the tears were coming down my face.

"Why are you crying? Is everything alright with you?"

"I just don't want the two of you to have to go through this again; I want the two of you to enjoy the life the both of you helped create."

"Stop crying Qort, everything is going to be fine, trust me, everything happens for a reason, so whatever the outcome may be, everything happens for a reason, so go get you something to eat, calm down and trust me, everything will be just fine," he told me while handing me money to go buy my food and Amber's stuff.

"Thank you Nathan, I don't know how you're holding up so well, but I truly thank you, not just for the pep talk, but for everything, making my cousin happy again, and being there for me whenever I needed, I appreciate it."

"That's what family is for."

I went down to the hospital's cafeteria and got me something light to eat, grabbed Amber's things she wanted, and I also picked up some magazines and things for all of us to look at because there was no telling how long we'd be at the hospital. Once I got back upstairs, I called my job and told them I was going to be out for a couple of days because of an emergency in the family. As I was leaving the cafeteria, I bumped into one of my neighbors and his cousin I believe he said his name was Tony. Tony was very easy on the eyes and for some reason I couldn't take my eyes off of him, and I think the feeling was mutual with him concerning me when we began talking.

"So, my cousin tells me that you two are in a relationship, does that mean you can't have friends?"

"I can have friends, but friend is a word I don't use too loosely, would you like to be an associate of mine? Maybe with time you can work your way to the 'friend' level."

"I like your style; maybe we can exchange numbers and maybe go out bowling or something one day."

"I'd like that, I'd like that a lot," I replied smiling like a little schoolgirl.

After exchanging numbers with Tony I decided to call Qamar because I knew it had been a while since he and Nathan had spoken to each other, and I thought it would be best that he come down to the hospital to show some support for his cousin during this time.

"Qamar, are you busy?"

"Nah, what's up shorty?"

"You need to come to the hospital and show some support for your cousin right now, that's what's up."

"Nah, it's been a minute since Nate and I talked and I'm not about to just come up there just because his shorty is in the hospital, that's not going to happen."

"You're such an insensitive asshole, you're cousin could possibly lose his child and you don't want to come here to show support? You're fucking ridiculous."

"Yo, watch ya mouth, you're not about to talk to me like I'm some little ass kid, him and I aren't on the best of terms and I'm not coming down there to act fake and act like I care about the situation him and his girl are in, not going to happen shorty. Now, answer me this, how long do you plan on being up there with them, I'm horny and I need some ass, pronto."

"You have issues and you better get acquainted with your hands because I'm not leaving this hospital until they discharge my cousin. You need a serious reality check, how can you be so selfish towards your cousin? He was the one that helped me when I suffered my miscarriage, oh wait, my bad, you were the insensitive bastard who caused me to have the miscarriage in the first place. Qamar, you have a lot of growing up to do still and I pray that if our child is a male he grows up to be absolutely nothing like you, one asshole like you is enough to last this world a lifetime," I told him right before hanging up right in his face.

"He's so damn insensitive it makes no sense, what do I see in him? He's only worried about himself, fuckin' selfish bastard," I said to myself aloud.

I walked back into Amber's room and she was asleep and Nathan was on the bed with her watching television. I threw a couple of sports magazines on his lap, and put the rest of the things I purchased on one of the tables in the room, then I laid down on the couch in the room, I was definitely starting to feel the effects of this pregnancy, I was starting to be tired all the time.

"Qort, why don't you go home and get some sleep, you need to be comfortable while sleeping and I know for damn sure you're not comfortable on that tight ass couch; if there are any changes with the situation I'll call you, aight?"

"I'm good Nate, I don't want to leave her, she helped me so much while I was going through, and I don't want to not reciprocate the gesture. She basically stopped all that she needed to do to ensure I was good until I was able to start getting around and doing for myself, I'm good right here."

He chuckled, "I know for sure the both of you are family, y'all are both stubborn, do you want me to at least see if they have a roll away bed for you to sleep on instead of the couch?"

"Nate, stop worrying so much, I'm fine!"

"Aight, cool. Umm, have you talked to ya man lately?"

"I called him while I was downstairs, I told him he needed to come down here to support you, but he was on some bitch shit and was like the both of you haven't spoken in a while and he's not about to be on some fake shit and come down here and support you."

"Wow, I don't even know how to take that."

"I cussed him out and told him that he was an insensitive bastard and then hung up on him; answer me this, what is it that I see in his ass? He's such a jerk, I can't stand it!"

"Only you know the answer to that question Qort, but don't stress over it, karma is going to come back on him, I mean I never would have thought that as close as him and I were when we were younger, we'd be this distant now, but I guess some things have to work themselves out, I'm not going to stress it and I don't want you stressing over it either, everything will come together in due time, trust."

"How do you continue to be so strong in a messed up time like this? I would be cracking at the seams if it were me, or if the shoes were on the other foot, I commend you, and I really do."

"Honestly? I'm a nervous wreck on the inside, I'm just keeping it together for the sake of Amber, if she sees me crack, then she'll crack and I don't want that."

"Respect, I feel you on that," I told him while fighting back a yawn.

"Go ahead and get some rest Qort, I can see it all in your eyes that you're past exhausted, you need to catch up on sleep before you get admitted into a room for extreme exhaustion."

"I know I'm going to get some sleep, wake me up if the doctor comes in or if anything happens."

"I will, you have my word."

Ten hours later

"Arrggghhh!"

"Amber, what's wrong? Are you alright?"

"No, I'm having contractions and I don't want to push, get my nurse or doctor in here now, please!"

My heart began pounding, I was scared out of my mind, I had an eerie feeling that my cousin was about to give birth to her five-month-old fetus, and I wasn't ready to witness that.

"Nurse! Nurse, I need someone in here now, my cousin is having contractions, she's about to give birth!"

The nurses and doctors all ran into the room, Doctor Jones, started prepping to examine her, I began crying, I called Nathan to tell him he needed to get back up to the hospital as soon as possible because his child could very well be born in the next few minutes.

Dr. Jones looked at me and said, "Qortni, I'm going to need for you to pull yourself together and help Amber through this, the contractions are coming too close together and she's going to have to deliver, I need you to be her support system right now, can you handle that?"

"Yes, I can handle that, what do you need me to do?"

"Hold her hand with one hand and hold her right leg up so she can push the baby out."

I did as Dr. Jones instructed me to do and after about two and a half pushes Amber gave birth to a cute five-month-old fetus, whom was breathing on his own.

"Qort, have you talked to Nathan? Did he say where he was at or when he'd be back up here?"

"Before I could respond to her questions, Nathan responded, "I'm right here baby, I apologize for missing the birth of our son, I didn't think me being gone for a few hours would mean me missing the birth, how are you doing?"

"I'm good babe, tired, but good."

"Doctor Jones, what are the chances of the baby surviving? I know babies aren't fully developed until their seven months old, and being that this little man right here was born at five months, what are his chances of living?" I asked the Doctor.

"Honestly, the odds of the baby living are slim to none, his lungs aren't fully developed as well as a lot of his other vital organs, I would say he has about another hour or so of living before his body realizes it can't function on its own, so my best advice to all of you is to get as much time with him now as possible because he's not going to make it."

I cried and left the room; I figured I'd give Nate and Amber some alone time with their first-born.

I called Qamar to see if he could come down to the hospital to lend some support and he denied, I was really starting to get aggravated by his lack of respect and support for his cousin, who was more like a brother to him, I mean even Nature came down to show his support and there were no family ties between the both of them.

Nathan stepped out of the room with tears in his eyes; I then knew that the baby had taken his last breath. I couldn't control my cries, I fell to the floor because I knew all to well the pain and heartache that goes along with losing a child.

Qamar and I are five months into our second pregnancy together and with each day that passes by I grow to hate him more and more; my parents are constantly getting on my nerves and I'm just tired of all three of them. On the other hand, Tony and I have been spending quality time together though we haven't slept together yet, mainly because he respects the fact that I'm in a relationship, he's a wonderful listener, he accepts me for me, even though I haven't yet told him that I'm pregnant, hopefully when I do things won't become awkward between us, I mean so far he seems as if that wouldn't faze him, but it's still too early to tell. Our first date we went bowling and I had a ton of fun he ended up beating me three games to two. After our date he brought me by his brother's house to meet his brother, and his brother seems really cool, I also met his sister and for some reason I get a real fake vibe from her, she just doesn't see, genuine, but it's nothing I have to worry about because I'm not dealing with Tony on an intimate level, we're strictly friends, nothing more, nothing less. I almost feel bad about not telling Tony I'm pregnant, but then again, my parents don't even know that I'm pregnant and I'm trying to keep it that way for at least another couple of weeks, I'm still trying to figure out the perfect way to tell them, we don't have the best relationship and I don't feel totally comfortable telling them that I'm pregnant, I don't feel comfortable talking to them about anything period, sad right?

Qamar decided that he wanted to do something special for me since he knows he's been being a butt hole lately, so he decided to book a room at one of the hotels at Foxwoods Casino for us, something sexy for me so he says, but in all honesty, I'm just not feeling the thought of going that far out of town with him, knowing that my mouth has been very reckless lately towards him, I don't trust him.

"So, what's the whole point of you getting this room for us?"

"We've both been stress lately, we've both been getting on each other's nerves lately and I wanted to do something for you to show you that I really do care about you. I want us to work; I want us to be a family when the baby comes Qortni."

As I was about to respond his phone began to ring, and I noticed Durriyah's name popped up on the screen an of course he ignored the call, then she texted him and me being me, I took his phone out of his hand and read the message.

"Hey Q, it's Durriyah, being that you didn't answer my call I can only assume that you're with you girl, hopefully you can respond to me when she's asleep or something, anyhow I appreciate you reaching out to me again, I bet Qortni would never guess that you and I are talking on a friendly level again, she's shit a brick if she found out, LOL. But I was calling you to let you know that I would gladly go to the casino with you next weekend, we haven't been out together since Qortni made you call me that day and tell me that you and I couldn't be friends any longer, it hurt my feelings because you're a cool dude and you're a great friend, but I won't keep you too long, just hit me back when you get a moment."

"So, you and this bitch taking weekend trips to the casino and shit? Since when are you and her back being friends after I told you that I didn't feel comfortable with that whole situation? This is the bullshit I'm talking about when I say you're constantly disrespecting this relationship and me. Have you and that bitch fucked? Better yet, I don't even want to know the answer to that, we can pack all our shit back up and bounce, I'm not staying here with you this weekend, bring me home please."

"Qortni, can we please talk about this?"

"There is nothing to talk about, now are you going to take me home or not?"

"Yes, I'll take you home, but trust this conversation is far from over."

"The conversation is over, and so is this relationship, I can't do this anymore, I'm tired of stressing, I'm tired of the disrespect, I'm tired of you Qamar, the sight of you makes me absolutely sick, I can't keep giving you chance after chance, I can be miserable by my damn self, I'm done for good, there's no coming back after this."

Ten minutes after our argument we were in his aunt's car on our way back to New Haven, I had officially had it with him and I was tired of the constant make up to break up charade him and I were playing, enough was enough.

What Qamar didn't know is that I already knew he had been creeping around with Durriyah for the past month, you see, my sister had called me one afternoon after Qamar had the balls to drive pass her house with that bitch in his front seat as if him and I weren't a couple and he didn't have a baby on the way, straight disrespecting. I kept that to myself because I knew he would end up fucking up and slipping, and sure enough, he slipped up tonight, dummy.

As we were pulling up to my house, I turned in my seat and looked him dead in his eyes and told him, "Qamar, you and I both know that shit between us has gone from okay to absolutely ridiculous in the time we've been together and there's no need in the both of us acting like we're happy because we both know that's an absolute lie, I can't keep dealing like this, being constantly unhappy, having you disrespect me like it okay, and acting like you being the asshole of the decade is just fine because it's not, things between us are so bad I've come to the point that I really hate you and that's not a good look at all, and I can't see myself having to deal with you for the duration of this pregnancy and even after the baby is born; I think I want to either give the baby up for adoption or I want you to sign over all of your parental rights."

"Qortni, you're out of your mind if you think I'm going to allow you to give my child up for adoption or even sign over my rights, that child is just as much apart of me as it is apart of you, I can't believe you have the gumption to ask me something like that, you're bugged the fuck out, and if you claim you have forgiven me for all the shit I have taken you through then why the fuck do you still constantly bring it up?"

"Why the fuck were you riding around with that bitch Durriyah in your car as if you don't have a girl and a baby on the way?"

His eyes grew as big as saucers I could tell he was trying to get his lies together.

"Qortni, who told you that bullshit, I would never disrespect you like that, you know me better than that," he told me avoiding all eye contact with me, which was a dead giveaway.

"If it's not true then how come I know what you had on that day as well as her? And please don't think I didn't peep her shades in your car, and her wallet, you fucking dummy. You're a dummy for having her in your car in the first place and she's the idiot for not realizing that she left her things in you car, especially her wallet that has her address on it."

"You will not go to her house starting any shit, do you hear me?"

"You're right, I'm not because as far as she's concerned she can have you because I've through!"

"Qort, I'm going to give you a couple of days to yourself to really think about what you're saying, you don't really want to leave me, you love me."

"Newsflash! I never loved you, I tolerated you, I was with you because you were something to do, someone to go out with so I wouldn't have to search through my phone log for a date to dinner or the movies, you were simply something to do, something to pass my time by, and our time together is up, I'm gone!"

As I was getting my bags and things out of the car Qamar was pleading with me to stay, and as I was taking my last bag out of the car, he asked me to get back into the car so he could talk to me, but as far as I was concerned, there was nothing left to talk about, he did his dirt, he was found out and now I was done with him for good.

"Qortni, can you just please hear me out? I'll only take ten minutes of your time, I promise."

"Hurry the hell up Qamar, my time is precious, too precious for you anymore," I told him while walking back towards the car.

When I got half way in the car, this jackass pulled off while I'm holding onto the door.

"Qamar, what the fuck are you doing? Stop the car!"

He kept speeding down the block, I had to make a decision, either allow him to kill me or I would have to let go of the door and pray to God no damage was going to be done to the baby I held in my stomach, I decided to let go because this fool wasn't thinking about stopping the car. When I let go of the car I fell hard onto the ground, stomach first, and I was pretty sure I had done some damage to my child, God knows I was hoping I didn't end up having another miscarriage. Once I got my bearings straight, I walked back to my house to get my car, this definitely meant war and pregnant or not, Qamar was about to make me whoop his ass one last time because the bullshit he just pulled was ridiculous and uncalled for, he was definitely about to pay.

Before going to his grandmother's house to whoop his ass I had to make a pit stop to Walgreens to buy some peroxide and gauze so I can patch myself up from the bruises and scrapes I managed to get. When I got near his house, I parked my car at my cousin's house and walked to his backyard and peeked through his bedroom window, this dummy was laying across his bed like he hadn't just tried to kill my unborn child and me.

I lifted his window without him hearing me and managed to get my pregnant ass in his room without noise, one good thing about what I was doing, he had his television volume up so high he couldn't hear anything. Once I got into his room I took one of his belts that were lying on the floor and hit him with it across his back, I wanted him to feel the shit I was going through.

"Qortni, what the fuck are you doing? How did you get in here and why the hell did you hit me with that damn belt?"

"Fuck you mean why did I hit you with the belt, why the fuck did you drag me down the street with your car? Are you out of your fucking mind? Did you forget that I'm carrying your child?"

"Qortni, listen to me, I only did it because you weren't trying to hear me out, did I get your attention?"

"You no good bastard, you do realize you could have killed me and my baby?"

"I didn't so stop stressing, now come lay down with me," he told me in the calmest voice.

I tilted my head to the left and looked at him as if he had lost his mind, because as far as I was concerned, he had done just that. Did he really just tell me to stop stressing and lay down with him?

"Wait, let me get this straight, you just tried to kill me and my child no less than an hour ago and now you want me to calm down and lay with you, yeah, you're officially crazy."

"Qortni, what do you want from me, I don't know what to do with you, so please tell me, what do you want from me?"

"I want you out of my life for the rest of my life, that's what I want, and I want you to sign over your parental rights to this baby, I don't want to have anything to do with you and I don't want you to have anything to do with my child, that's what I want. Being that you couldn't be trustworthy and committed I don't want anything else to do with you."

"Qortni, can I have just one more chance? I promise to do better if you give me just one more chance, baby please?"

"Your 'one more chance' options are all used up, those tickets are sold, burned and can't be put pack together, I can't do it anymore, if I keep giving you chance after chance I'm going to die giving you chances, I can't keep putting myself through the same bullshit again time after time with you, our relationship has run its course, there's nothing left, we need to count our blessings for us breaking up and just move on."

He stood in the middle of his room and just stared at me, then out of nowhere just jumped on me and began choking me. I don't know where the burst of energy came from but I was able to push him off of me and run to the front of his grandmother's house and out the front door. I thought I had escaped him, but he jumped out of his room window and when I got to my car, he was knelt down trying to slash my tires with a dull steak knife.

"So after you choke me you're going to slash my tires?"

"Yea, I'm tired of you acting like you don't love me so I'm slashing your tires to ensure you don't go anywhere."

"How about you allow me to show you how to really slash tires," I told him opening up my trunk and grabbing my duffle bag. I walked back to his back yard and pulled out one of my favorite knives and slashed all four of his tires, then opened his car door and took my knife to all of his seats; just as I was closing his car door his grandmother came out speaking in her heavy Jamaican accent to me probably cussing me out all the while waving a knife at me.

I told the old lady, "If you use that knife on me you better kill me with it because if you don't, you're going to regret coming at me with that damn knife."

"You leave my grandson's car alone! You're nothing but trouble, can't stand you, never could, you better leave here before I call the police," she ranted still shaking the knife in my direction.

"I don't really give a damn about you not liking me, I don't like you either, never did, now your best bet is to go back in the house and go sit and rock in your rocking chair, this shit out here has nothing to do with you at all, it's between your grandson and I."

"You yellow bitch, you touch my grandson and I'm going to kill you!"

"You try and you're going to meet your maker sooner than later, now step off grandma!" I told her.

"Now you're threatening my grandmother?" Qamar asked me.

"No I'm not threatening her, I'm promising her what will happen to her if she tries to use that knife on me," I told him before suddenly feeling something warm coming down my legs. I couldn't tell if it was blood because I had on dark velour sweatpants, but I knew for damn sure I wasn't peeing on myself.

"Qamar, I'm done with you, whatever things of mine I have in your room, please bring to my house whenever you get a chance, I can't do this anymore, tired of wasting time and energy with you."

I surprisingly walked down his driveway without him on my heels got in my car and headed to Amberlin's house. I called Amberlin while I was on my way over there to let her know I was coming and what had happened.

When I got to her house I noticed a big dark stain on my car seat, and I could tell it wasn't urine, which only meant I was bleeding. I used my key to get in to her house and I made a beeline to her guest bathroom, I always kept at least two extra outfits at her house.

"Qortni, are you alright? There are spots of blood on my floor, where are you bleeding from?"

"I think I'm having a miscarriage, the blood won't stop, my car seat is full of blood, and honestly, I don't know if I want to even try to save the baby this time around."

"I'm taking you to the hospital right now, no questions asked, let's go!"

Before I was able to respond to Amber, my phone rang, it was Tony."

Before I answered his call I had to compose myself, "Hey sweetie what's going on?"

"Nothing much ma, chilling here, thinking about you. Everything all right with you there, I'm sensing something is wrong?"

Tony lived in New Jersey, and when him and I met, he was up here visiting family and his two daughters that lived up here. I sometimes took day trips down there to see him and hit up the mall.

"Everything is cool, I'm at my cousins house right now, her and I are about to go out for a little while."

"Qort, something isn't right, I can hear it all in your voice, now be real with me, what's going on?"

I began crying, I don't know what it was about Tony but he could always sense when something wasn't right with me, even if I was over the phone with him, I could never hide my emotions from him.

I began crying and said, "Qamar and I had a huge fight, he dragged me down the street with his car and I went and whooped his ass, now I'm bleeding and I think I may be having a miscarriage but I don't want to go to the hospital right now, I honestly don't want to save this baby, I don't want to be tied to him at all, by no means necessary, I just want this nightmare of a relationship to end."

As Tony and I were engaged in our conversation Amber and I were in her car on our way to the hospital so I could get checked out, even though we both pretty much already knew what the outcome was.

"Qortni listen to me please, let your cousin take you to the hospital so you can get checked out, the last thing I want to happen to you is for you to be losing too much blood because of the miscarriage, then I want your cousin to come pick me up from the train station, I'm going to pay ole boy a visit, then once you're cleared from the hospital I want you to come to Jersey with me for a few days."

"Tony I need to handle this myself; I don't want you getting caught up in my battles. You're not even supposed to be leaving the state, I don't want you to come up here, do something crazy and land yourself back in jail, I wouldn't feel right having that happen to you. After I get checked out at the hospital and get cleared, I'll come stay with you for a couple of days, retail therapy will be just what I need to get over all of this bullshit."

"I'll be down there this weekend Qort, you're coming back to Jersey with me after that, call me in the morning or after you come from the hospital, either way call me, no matter the time, just call me to let me know you're all right."

"Okay sweetie, I'll call you."

"Sounds like you and Tony are pretty serious."

"No, just good friends, I can talk to him about anything, he's been my shoulder to cry on and listening ear since we've met, he's a real good guy, someone I need in my corner," I responded to her while starting out the car window.

"Good guys and real friends are hard to come by, just make sure he doesn't become a rebound guy for you, I don't want you getting your heart broken by him, then I'll have to kick his ass."

Once we got to the hospital one of the emergency room technicians wheeled me directly up to the fourth floor of the hospital, the labor and delivery unit. I was then taken into one of the triage rooms where one of the mid-wives on duty came in to check me, and as suspected, I lost the baby, even though the fetus was still in me, I had to push it out still.

After I delivered my still born baby I was taken into a room that I would be staying in for about another day or so before I was released from the hospital, and after getting settled into my room there was a knock on my door.

"Come in," I told whomever it was knockin on my room door.

When my door opened, I almost passed out; they were guests I definitely wasn't expecting to see in my room.

"Are you Ms. Qortni Monroe?" the short one asked.

"Yes, I'm she, is there something I can help you officers with?" I asked with the most perplexed look on my face.

"Ms. Monroe, we have a warrant for your arrest, we need you to get dressed and come down to the police station with us so you can give us your statement about what happened between you and Mr. Daniels tonight."

"Statement? Arrest warrants? Are you kidding me? I just gave birth and you're coming up in here to arrest me and make me give a statement? He really called the cops on me?"

"Any and all questions can be answered down at the station ma'am, now can you please get dressed and come with us?"

Amber began crying her eyes out, I was just a bit stunned, but I shed no tears, I couldn't, I was numb to the pain Qamar kept throwing at me, in fact, I thought this whole event of the night was pretty funny, especially him calling the cops on me after he dragged me down the street knowing I was pregnant.

I began getting dressed and I told Amber to call Tony to let him know what was going on and I instructed her to meet me at the courthouse in the morning, thankfully today is Thursday, so there will be no spending the weekend in lock up for me, good thinking on my part right?

The police officers read me my Miranda rights, cuffed me and once we got outside of the hospital they placed me in the paddy wagon. Once the officers rounded up everyone that was wanted that evening in the paddy wagon we all made our way to the main police station on Union Avenue. Once we got out we were all searched by one of the judicial marshal's at the jail and then placed into a cell, and me being me, I gave the female marshal a tough time because she was purposely roughly searching me like she had something against me and I didn't know this woman from a can of paint, long story short, she wasn't the only one who was leaving bruised up, I made sure she felt my wrath.

I didn't bother making my one phone call, I mean it was pointless, no one at my parent's house was going to answer the phone and I know for damn sure no one was going to bail me out, trifling right? Instead of crying like a punk and being mad at Qamar for me being locked up, I started to reflect on my life over the past few years and how I needed to change things and quickly before I ended up either doing jail time or in the ground six feet under.

Friday Morning

I couldn't sleep for shit last night I mean how could I? Did they really expect people to sleep in a cold ass cell on metal beds with no cushion, blankets or pillows? Did they really expect me to pee in a cell where there was no privacy, copping a squat in front of the other two hundred or more people in cells around me? I think not, I was up all night reflecting on my life and came to the conclusion that my life and sanity are far more important than being miserable and going through miscarriage after miscarriage with Qamar, so I was officially done with him, there was no looking back, no turning back, I'd be a fool to. Around nine o'clock the marshal's opened up the cells and allowed us to make a couple of phone calls to see if we could get someone to bail us out so we wouldn't have to go to court, but of course, all the phones at my parents house blocked calls from jails, and the only number I was able to get through to was my aunt's office number, but of course just because I needed her she wasn't in her office, but I guess it didn't matter because I'm pretty sure she didn't have five thousand dollars laying around to bail me out, so off to court I went. After all who wanted to make calls did, the marshal's handcuffed all of our hands and shackled all of our feet together two by two before we got into the van to be transported to the courthouse.

Once we got to the courthouse we were all brought to the basement where they had holding cells so we could wait for our cases to be called or for attorney's or counselor's to come and talk to us, in my case a state counselor for domestic cases came and talked to me, but I really wasn't trying to hear her, I mean not for nothing, I knew I needed to get out of the situation I was in, so her words were going in one ear and out the other with me, that was until she told me that my older brother was in the court room waiting for my case to be called, that's when my ears perked up, my heart started racing and the tears began to freely fall from my eyes.

"Ms. Monroe, why are you crying all of a sudden? Is it something I said?"

"I can't allow my brother to see me like this, my hair is a mess, I'm cuffed at the wrists, my feet are shackled, this is not how I want him to see me, he can't see me like this."

"He's in some type of uniform, what does he do for a living?"

"He's a correction officer for the state, he sees others like this on a daily basis, he can't see his little sister like this, it's just not right."

"You'll be alright, I promise you, since this is your first offense you'll get a PTA and maybe a year of probation, and they'll probably try to get you to go to anger management classes or something, but you won't be doing any jail time, very rarely does that happen to those who are first offenders."

I nodded my head and went back to my holding cell to wait for my case to be called. As I walked into the courtroom I locked eyes with my brother and my heart sank, I felt like I let him down, I felt like a failure, I felt like shit. When I stood up in front of the judge as the marshal ran down my charges I said a silent prayer that he would let me off with a promise to appear and probation, I couldn't go to jail for whooping Qamar's ass, I'm too pretty for jail, I might get turned out, because fucking with Qamar for this long, I actually forgot what good, strong dick felt like.

"Ms. Monroe, I'm going to give you a later date to appear in court, and I would advise you not to miss that court date or there will be a warrant out for your arrest, do you understand me?"

"Yes your honor, I understand."

"Good, now since Mr. Daniels has decided not to press charges on you, I have to ask you if you would like to press charges against him, but before you answer I must warn you that if you do in fact press charges against him the both of you will be facing jail time, now do you wish to press charges against Mr. Daniels?"

"No your Honor, I'll wave all charges that are against him."

"Very well then, you are free to go and you need to be back in court a month from Monday," the judge responded then banged his gavel against the sounding block and had the marshal call the next case.

I was taken to the side of the courtroom where the marshals could un-cuffed me and unshackled my feet, then my brother met me outside.

"Qort, dad is on the phone for you," my brother told me.

I took the phone from his hand and promptly pressed the *end* button, my father was one person I wasn't in the mood to be talking to right now. As my brother and I were walking down the stairs of the courthouse waiting for my brother in law to circle the block to bring us home, my brother asked me what happened, since he had just found out about it only hours earlier when he was getting off work. I gave him the whole run down of the previous nights events, and I ended the conversation by telling him that I didn't regret anything I did, if I had to do it all over again I would in a heartbeat.

Once I got home, I was greeted by my aunt, which explained why she hadn't answered her work phone when I tried to call her earlier; anyhow, she embraced me in a hug and asked me if I was all right, I told her I was and then made my way up to where my room was so I could take a warm bath.

As I was running my bath water I put Epsom salt in the water because my joints were aching, very bad move because I totally forgot about all of the bruises I had all over because of the bullshit I endured last night, needless to say, I made that bath a very quick one, then laid down for a couple of hours before I headed to my younger brother's football game.

After about four hours of sleeping my ringing cell phone woke me up, it was my brother in law calling to see if I was driving to the game myself or if I was riding with him and my brother and of course I told him I was riding, I wasn't really in the mood to be behind the wheel, I need to relax still.

An hour after the game

When I got home from the game, which in fact my brother's team won, I noticed my personal room phone had fifteen missed calls, some of which were from Quetta, some were from Tony and most of them were from Qamar's aggravating ass. I decided to call Quetta back in the morning, but I was definitely going to return Tony's phone calls, he had a strange way of making me feel as if everything was going to be all right.

"Qortni, are you all right? You had me worried."

"I'm fine Tony, I'm home, I'm good; how are you?"

"I'm better now that I'm on the phone with you, what happened to you? It's not like you to not return my phone calls; did I do or say something to upset you?"

"No you didn't, I got arrested last night, long story, I'll fill you in on everything that happened next time I see you," I told him not really wanting to have to explain again the events of last night, I did enough of that already today with too many people.

Tony and I talked for a good two hours on the phone before I decided to call it a night; I was mentally and physically exhausted. Just as I was about to fall into a deep sleep, my house phone rang, and I honestly thought it was Tony calling back to mess with me, so I answered it.

"I thought I told you I was going to call you back in the morning after I got myself together, what? You just had to hear my voice one more time before you went to sleep?

"Why the fuck didn't you answer any of my calls? Where the hell were you?" Do you not remember that you need to check in with me when you go out? What the hell is wrong with you?"

It wasn't Tony on the other line of the phone; it was Qamar, so I calmly responded, "Qamar, you do realize that the events of last night ended out relationship right? We are no longer a couple, we're done and over with! Get it through your head that Qortni and Qamar are no longer a couple! I want and need you to understand that besides the fact that the lives you gave me are the same lives you took away from me, I can't deal with you any longer or I'm going to lose my sanity. I'm happy not being with you, this has not worked for us since we got together, I never checked in with you, you never had me on a rope like that, now please refrain from calling me any longer as I may be inclined to call the cops on your ass this time around," I told him then hung up the phone before he had a chance to respond...

"THEY SAY I'M A WOMAN of many talents, which is true, my only problem was figuring out which talent(s) I wanted to pursue full time." - **ROCKY ROSE**

Rocky Rose was born and raised in New Haven, CT. Rocky began to perfect her writing style and seriously value her ability her sophomore year in high school. Only after her English teacher noticed and expressed to Rocky how much talent Rocky had did she begin to believe. Rocky's story, which was read by many of her friends in high school, proved that her imagination was phenomenal, and that she could create wonderful images and scenarios in her mind first, then on paper. Writing was not only fun for Rocky; it also served as an outlet for her emotions. She never had the type of relationship with her parents where she could talk to them about anything so she wrote down her feelings instead. Even though writing came naturally to her, Rocky never once thought about pursuing a writing career until 2005 when she enrolled into the *Breaking Into Print* writing program, where she completed the course and received her diploma in just two years.

In November of 2010, Rocky met her mentor and sister, Karen E. Quinones Miller, who told Rocky that she had *raw* talent. Rocky began writing her first novel, *My Man My Abuser*, which is about three years of her life in which she was in a domestically violent relationship. In 2012 Rocky wrote *I Win You Lose*, which is a compilation of six short stories dealing with Domestic Violence.

When Rocky isn't writing she enjoys spending time with her daughter and son, going bowling, to the movies and shooting pool. Rocky resides in New Haven, CT with her daughter and son.